Test Prep & Admissions Consulting

Turbocharge your GMAT:
Analytical Writing Guide

part of the 6th Edition Series

April 20th, 2016

- ☐ *Essay on real AWA topics*
- ☐ *Comprehensive strategies to write a 6.0 essay*
- ☐ *Emphasis on 'How to ideate'*
- ☐ *Structured approach to brainstorm essay prompt*
- ☐ *Detailed 4-step process for a 30-minute AWA task*
- ☐ *Tips on improving vocabulary and language*
- ☐ *Two essays with 4 versions (scored 6/5/3/2)*
- ☐ *40 sample essays and their critique*

www.manhattanreview.com

Copyright and Terms of Use

Copyright and Trademark

All materials herein (including names, terms, trademarks, designs, images, and graphics) are the property of Manhattan Review, except where otherwise noted. Except as permitted herein, no such material may be copied, reproduced, displayed or transmitted or otherwise used without the prior written permission of Manhattan Review. You are permitted to use material herein for your personal, noncommercial use, provided that you do not combine such material into a combination, collection, or compilation of material. If you have any questions regarding the use of the material, please contact Manhattan Review at info@manhattanreview.com.

This material may make reference to countries and persons. The use of such references is for hypothetical and demonstrative purposes only.

Terms of Use

By using this material, you acknowledge and agree to the terms of use contained herein.

No Warranties

This material is provided without warranty, either express or implied, including the implied warranties of merchantability, of fitness for a particular purpose and noninfringement. Manhattan Review does not warrant or make any representations regarding the use, accuracy or results of the use of this material. This material may make reference to other source materials. Manhattan Review is not responsible in any respect for the content of such other source materials, and disclaims all warranties and liabilities with respect to the other source materials.

Limitation on Liability

Manhattan Review shall not be responsible under any circumstances for any direct, indirect, special, punitive, or consequential damages ("Damages") that may arise from the use of this material. In addition, Manhattan Review does not guarantee the accuracy or completeness of its course materials, which are provided "as is" with no warranty, express or implied. Manhattan Review assumes no liability for any Damages from errors or omissions in the material, whether arising in contract, tort or otherwise.

10-Digit International Standard Book Number: (ISBN: 1-62926-071-1)
13-Digit International Standard Book Number: (ISBN: 978-1-62926-071-6)

Last updated on April 20th, 2016.

Manhattan Review, 275 Madison Avenue, Suite 1429, New York, NY 10016.
Phone: +1 (212) 316-2000. E-Mail: info@manhattanreview.com. Web: www.manhattanreview.com

About the Turbocharge your GMAT Series

The Turbocharge Your GMAT Series is carefully designed to be clear, comprehensive, and content-driven. Long regarded as the gold standard in GMAT prep worldwide, Manhattan Review's GMAT prep books offer professional GMAT instruction for dramatic score improvement. Now in its updated 6th edition, the full series is designed to provide GMAT test-takers with complete guidance for highly successful outcomes. As many students have discovered, Manhattan Review's GMAT books break down the different test sections in a coherent, concise, and accessible manner. We delve deeply into the content of every single testing area and zero in on exactly what you need to know to raise your score. The full series is comprised of 16 guides that cover concepts in mathematics and grammar from the most basic through the most advanced levels, making them a great study resource for all stages of GMAT preparation. Students who work through all of our books benefit from a substantial boost to their GMAT knowledge and develop a thorough and strategic approach to taking the GMAT.

- ☐ GMAT Math Essentials (ISBN: 978-1-62926-057-0)
- ☐ GMAT Number Properties Guide (ISBN: 978-1-62926-058-7)
- ☐ GMAT Arithmetics Guide (ISBN: 978-1-62926-059-4)
- ☐ GMAT Algebra Guide (ISBN: 978-1-62926-060-0)
- ☐ GMAT Geometry Guide (ISBN: 978-1-62926-061-7)
- ☐ GMAT Word Problems Guide (ISBN: 978-1-62926-062-4)
- ☐ GMAT Sets & Statistics Guide (ISBN: 978-1-62926-063-1)
- ☐ GMAT Combinatorics & Probability Guide (ISBN: 978-1-62926-064-8)
- ☐ GMAT Data Sufficiency Guide (ISBN: 978-1-62926-065-5)
- ☐ GMAT Quantitative Question Bank (ISBN: 978-1-62926-066-2)
- ☐ GMAT Sentence Correction Guide (ISBN: 978-1-62926-067-9)
- ☐ GMAT Critical Reasoning Guide (ISBN: 978-1-62926-068-6)
- ☐ GMAT Reading Comprehension Guide (ISBN: 978-1-62926-069-3)
- ☐ GMAT Integrated Reasoning Guide (ISBN: 978-1-62926-070-9)
- ■ GMAT Analytical Writing Guide (ISBN: 978-1-62926-071-6)
- ☐ GMAT Vocabulary Builder (ISBN: 978-1-62926-072-3)

About the Company

Manhattan Review's origin can be traced directly back to an Ivy League MBA classroom in 1999. While teaching advanced quantitative subjects to MBAs at Columbia Business School in New York City, Professor Dr. Joern Meissner developed a reputation for explaining complicated concepts in an understandable way. Remembering their own less-than-optimal experiences preparing for the GMAT, Prof. Meissner's students challenged him to assist their friends, who were frustrated with conventional GMAT preparation options. In response, Prof. Meissner created original lectures that focused on presenting GMAT content in a simplified and intelligible manner, a method vastly different from the voluminous memorization and so-called tricks commonly offered by others. The new approach immediately proved highly popular with GMAT students, inspiring the birth of Manhattan Review.

Since its founding, Manhattan Review has grown into a multi-national educational services firm, focusing on GMAT preparation, MBA admissions consulting, and application advisory services, with thousands of highly satisfied students all over the world. The original lectures have been continuously expanded and updated by the Manhattan Review team, an enthusiastic group of master GMAT professionals and senior academics. Our team ensures that Manhattan Review offers the most time-efficient and cost-effective preparation available for the GMAT. Please visit www.ManhattanReview.com for further details.

About the Founder

Professor Dr. Joern Meissner has more than 25 years of teaching experience at the graduate and undergraduate levels. He is the founder of Manhattan Review, a worldwide leader in test prep services, and he created the original lectures for its first GMAT preparation class. Prof. Meissner is a graduate of Columbia Business School in New York City, where he received a PhD in Management Science. He has since served on the faculties of prestigious business schools in the United Kingdom and Germany. He is a recognized authority in the areas of supply chain management, logistics, and pricing strategy. Prof. Meissner thoroughly enjoys his research, but he believes that grasping an idea is only half of the fun. Conveying knowledge to others is even more fulfilling. This philosophy was crucial to the establishment of Manhattan Review, and remains its most cherished principle.

The Advantages of Using Manhattan Review

▶ **Time efficiency and cost effectiveness.**

- For most people, the most limiting factor of test preparation is time.

- It takes significantly more teaching experience to prepare a student in less time.

- Our test preparation approach is tailored for busy professionals. We will teach you what you need to know in the least amount of time.

▶ **Our high-quality and dedicated instructors are committed to helping every student reach her/his goals.**

International Phone Numbers and Official Manhattan Review Websites

Manhattan Headquarters	+1-212-316-2000	www.manhattanreview.com
USA & Canada	+1-800-246-4600	www.manhattanreview.com
Argentina	+1-212-316-2000	www.review.com.ar
Australia	+61-3-9001-6618	www.manhattanreview.com
Austria	+43-720-115-549	www.review.at
Belgium	+32-2-808-5163	www.manhattanreview.be
Brazil	+1-212-316-2000	www.manhattanreview.com.br
Chile	+1-212-316-2000	www.manhattanreview.cl
China	+86-20-2910-1913	www.manhattanreview.cn
Czech Republic	+1-212-316-2000	www.review.cz
France	+33-1-8488-4204	www.review.fr
Germany	+49-89-3803-8856	www.review.de
Greece	+1-212-316-2000	www.review.com.gr
Hong Kong	+852-5808-2704	www.review.hk
Hungary	+1-212-316-2000	www.review.co.hu
India	+1-212-316-2000	www.review.in
Indonesia	+1-212-316-2000	www.manhattanreview.id
Ireland	+1-212-316-2000	www.gmat.ie
Italy	+39-06-9338-7617	www.manhattanreview.it
Japan	+81-3-4589-5125	www.manhattanreview.jp
Malaysia	+1-212-316-2000	www.review.my
Mexico	+1-212-316-2000	www.manhattanreview.mx
Netherlands	+31-20-808-4399	www.manhattanreview.nl
New Zealand	+1-212-316-2000	www.review.co.nz
Philippines	+1-212-316-2000	www.review.ph
Poland	+1-212-316-2000	www.review.pl
Portugal	+1-212-316-2000	www.review.pt
Qatar	+1-212-316-2000	www.review.qa
Russia	+1-212-316-2000	www.manhattanreview.ru
Singapore	+65-3158-2571	www.gmat.sg
South Africa	+1-212-316-2000	www.manhattanreview.co.za
South Korea	+1-212-316-2000	www.manhattanreview.kr
Sweden	+1-212-316-2000	www.gmat.se
Spain	+34-911-876-504	www.review.es
Switzerland	+41-435-080-991	www.review.ch
Taiwan	+1-212-316-2000	www.gmat.tw
Thailand	+66-6-0003-5529	www.manhattanreview.com
Turkey	+1-212-316-2000	www.review.com.tr
United Arab Emirates	+1-212-316-2000	www.manhattanreview.ae
United Kingdom	+44-20-7060-9800	www.manhattanreview.co.uk
Rest of World	+1-212-316-2000	www.manhattanreview.com

Contents

Chapter 1

Welcome

Dear Students,

At Manhattan Review, we constantly strive to provide the best educational content for preparation of standardized tests, putting arduous effort into making the best product possible. This continuous evolution is very important for an examination like the GMAT, which also evolves constantly. Sadly, a GMAT aspirant is often confused by too many study guide options in the market. The challenge is how to choose the book or tutor that will get you to your goal. Without saying that we are the best, we leave it for you to judge.

This book differs in many aspects from standard AWA books available on the market. Unlike AWA books from other prep companies, this book is comprehensive. It includes detailed theory; explanation on how to ideate; a detailed 4-step process for a 30-minute AWA task; a template for essay writing; a couple of essays with four versions (scored 6/5/3/2), along with their critiques; and 40 argumentative essays.

In a nut shell, Manhattan Review's GMAT-AWA guide is holistic and comprehensive in all respects. It has been created this way because we listen to what students need. Should you have any query, please feel free to write to us at *info@manhattanreview.com*.

Happy Learning!

Professor Dr. Joern Meissner
& The Manhattan Review Team

Chapter 2

Introduction to the GMAT AWA Task

The first section on the GMAT is possibly the one with most polarizing opinions – The Analytical Writing Assessment, aka the AWA.

Some people actually look forward to presenting their thoughts on paper, while others are terrified by the thought. However, to master the AWA task, all one needs is structured thinking and a good grasp of the English language.

2.1 What is the argument essay?

Essentially, the test taker is given 30 minutes to type an analytical essay, critiquing and evaluating a flawed argument (along the lines of a CR Weaken argument).

Note that the AWA score is not factored into the general GMAT score out of 800. This is a separate score, awarded on a scale of 0 to 6, moving in half-point increments (that is, 0 – 0.5 – 1 – 1.5, etc). Both a computer and a human (or two) will evaluate and grade your essay, and you'll receive your AWA score along with your official scores from GMAC, any time within 15 days of taking the exam.

2.2 How important are the AWA scores?

The AWA Task is not to be taken lightly. First of all, the way you attempt the task, in a smooth or bumpy manner, will set the tone for the rest of your test-taking experience. So, the attempt should be carefully planned and prepared for. The second point is the AWA score. Almost all business schools have their specific cut-offs not just for the GMAT general score (out of 800), but also for the AWA score (out of 6). The cut-offs range from 4 to 4.5; therefore, you should aim for 4.5 or above to be safe.

According to the scoring guide provided in the Official Guide,

"A _6.0 essay_ **presents a cogent, well-articulated critique of the argument and demonstrates mastery of the elements of effective writing**," though there may still be minor flaws, while, on the other hand, _No score_ means you've left the essay blank, written something off topic or in a language other than English (including gibberish), or just recopied the topic. So, to get a

0.0, one has to deliberately sabotage the AWA attempt.

To understand how important the AWA score is, let's look at the scores and corresponding percentiles, as well as the percentage of test-takers who got a particular score.

AWA Score Label Percentile

AWA Score	Label	Percentile	Percentage who score
6.0	Outstanding	91	9
5.5		77	14
5.0	Strong	57	20
4.5		38	19
4.0	Adequate	20	18
3.5		10	10
3.0	Limited	6	4
2.5		4	2
2.0	Seriously Flawed	3	1
1.5		3	0
1.0	Fundamentally Deficient	3	0
0.5		3	0
0	No score	0	3

Note that 80% of test-takers score "adequate" (4.0) or better, and nearly a half (43%) manage to get "strong" (5.0) or better.

These figures indicate that a great AWA score will not necessarily offset your GMAT score, especially if the general GMAT score (out of 800) is low. However, a bad AWA score (below 4.0) will definitely hamper your chances of admissions, even if you have a superb general GMAT score (out of 800). The purpose of the AWA is to help business schools cull the bottom 20% of candidates – the ones who cannot write English well-enough to manage graduate-level curriculum, or are not structured in their thinking or their approach, or are simply not serious about the process.

Therefore, your aim in the AWA is only to acquire a 4.5 or higher. In fact, even if you get a 4.0 (adequate), don't bother attempting the GMAT again just to improve the AWA score, since schools are fine with 4.0 or higher.

A seemingly scary fact is that schools can choose to read your essay, but it's not likely that they will. In fact, they almost certainly won't, given the amount of work that they have during the admissions process. They may read the essay of those who score low but are still in consideration for a seat. Also, be reassured that schools know that you have only 30 minutes in which to write the essay, and they realize that it represents a first draft of sorts.

2.3 What does the AWA specifically want?

The three main things that the AWA task is scored on are:

(1) **Organization and presentation** - How you present your thoughts: coherently or haphazardly

(2) **Logical analysis** - The quality of your ideas and points: whether the flaws you find are important or flimsy

(3) **Linguistic skills** - The level of your writing: persuasive or flawed

The essay task is described in Chapter 11 of The Official Guide for GMAT Review, 13th Edition. The chapter also includes a description of different scores and some example essays with different scores. The material is worth reading at least once. Also, right after the sample essays, the OG provides the complete pool of AWA questions that could appear on your exam. This is also the pool that is put up on mba.com* and contains all possible AWA questions. The number of AWA questions is around 135, but there is no need to practice writing all of them. Once you know how to organize your essay, how to brainstorm for ideas, and how to present your thoughts on paper, practice writing some essays and just read the remaining AWA prompts, as well as the sample essays in the subsequent chapters. That should be enough for you to get a high score on the AWA section.

The task contains an argument followed by a prompt. The AWA's argument contains a conclusion and premises, as you've learned in Critical Reasoning. In fact, your Critical Reasoning learning will help you in writing the essay. The argument that you need to analyze will contain a faulty conclusion based on insufficient premises. The prompt remains the same for any argument.

While there is no prescribed word limit, based on the various 6-score essays, the limit is from 300-600. That is not to say that you should aim to write up to 600 words. The limit is to suggest that writing fewer than 300 and more than 600 words is not recommended.

2.4 How does the GMAT program operate in the AWA?

A text box on part of the screen is the space in which you have to type your essay response. There is no limit to how much text you can enter, but the text box cannot be resized. That is, once you have entered about 9-11 lines, you will have to scroll up or down to read what you have written. The whole program looks very much like the Notepad application, with absolutely no formatting functions such as bold or italics, etc. Don't try to emphasize any particular part of your essay response using all caps or asterisks or any such keyboard-based trick. Let the sharpness of your essay persuade the reader.

You can use the following keyboard shortcuts when you are editing your essay.

Combination	Function	Description
Ctrl-X or Alt-T	Cut	Cuts text and puts it on a clipboard
Ctrl-C or Alt-C	Copy	Copies text onto the clipboard
Ctrl-V or Alt-P	Paste	Pastes text from the clipboard
Ctrl-Z or Alt-U	Undo	Undoes the last edit you made. You can undo only your last 10 edits.
Ctrl-Y or Alt-R	Redo	Redoes something you just undid. You can redo only the last 10 undone actions.

Apart from these keyboard combinations, the navigation keys on the keyboard have their standard function for moving the cursor up, down, left, or right. The enter and return keys insert a paragraph break and move you to a new line.

Page up and page down retain their standard function of moving the cursor up or down one screen. The keyboard also allows the standard functions of the backspace and delete buttons, and the home and end buttons,too, have their functions.

Tab or indent is not allowed. To make a new paragraph, just press enter a couple of times to put a blank space between paragraphs. If you prefer putting indentations at the start of new paragraphs, just hit the space bar a preset number of times, say 5 times for every new paragraph, to create a consistent indenting effect.

Like Notepad, the AWA program does not contain a spell check option. You have to rely on your own grammar and spelling skills. You would obviously not make any spelling or grammar mistakes deliberately, so, to ensure the fewest number of errors, practice multiple AWA essays in the Notepad application to see your spelling mistakes. Always carve out the last couple of minutes of the test to edit your essay and weed out the errors.

2.5   How to use the 30 minutes?

You are given exactly 30 minutes to do all you can with the particular AWA task given to you. The best way to avoid an unpleasant experience is to have a time-based plan and stick to it. Here is a plan for your 30 minutes:

(1) **2 minutes: Read**. Read the task carefully. Doing so will kick your brain into thinking mode and help you to focus on the task at hand and calm the butterflies in your stomach. In these 2 minutes, read the AWA question at least twice to ensure that you don't miss out on any nuance that you can exploit in your essay. In this part, you should break down the argument into the main conclusion and supporting premises so that you can start work on weakening the assumptions and evidence in the next part.

(2) **5 minutes: Ideate**. Here you will brainstorm and generate ideas in the manner discussed in Chapter 2. This part will generate the main thrust of your essay, so don't rush yourself, and remember to stick to the plan. This part should also yield a rough structure of what points you will mention in your essay – the four paragraphs. Divide the ideas into two main body paragraphs to allow faster typing in the next part.

(3) **20 minutes: Type.** This part is where you will use the general template discussed in the next chapter and flesh it out using the points you generated in the previous 5 minutes. If you are hit by writer's block, don't force yourself to go in a linear fashion. Type out whatever points occur to you, and then at every pause make sure you have arranged the points in proper order. By the end of this part, you should have a draft of your essay. To hit around 500 words, you should have written about 30-35 sentences of 15-20 words each. With sufficient practice, your essays will reach the desired mark and you will not have to actually count the number of words on the day of your exam.

(4) **3 minutes: Review.** At this point, resist the temptation to add any new points. Just read your essay twice, correcting it for grammar and spelling mistakes as you read, and ensure that proper transition words have been used as you switch from one point to the next. Also, try to increase the vocabulary level, but don't try to use fancy language, flowery words, or quotes/sayings. Stick to formal English and keep the language relevant and unornamented.

2.6 General tips

(1) After having read the full book, practice writing at least 4-5 essays.

(2) You can use the GMAT Write tool provided by GMAC.

(3) Go through the remaining AWA topics in the pool and think about what you would generally write about them.

(4) In your final 3-4 full-length tests, do the AWA part too, to get the full experience.

(5) Check your typing speed – it is better to write essays closer to 550-600 words than just 300 or so. You should be able to type that many words in less than 20 minutes.

(6) Absorb the vocabulary used in the 40 sample essays provided in the book, as well as in the vocabulary section in the next chapter. You should be familiar enough with these to incorporate them into your essay without any hassles.

(7) Read the sample essays more than once to train your mind to think along those lines.

(8) If your command on English is not strong, make sure you adhere to the principles you learn in Sentence Correction to minimize grammar errors. Reading quality publications such as The Economist or The New Yorker, among others, may help you to familiarize yourself with excellent English.

For the complete list of possible topics, please find the current link to download them for free here:

www.manhattanreview.com/gmat-analytical-writing-assessment/

Chapter 3

How to Write

3.1 The AWA Task

From the previous chapter, you already know what the AWA specifically grades you on. Now let's get into an actual AWA task to understand how to write it.

Let's look at an actual example from the Official Guide.

> *The following appeared in an announcement issued by the publisher of The Mercury, a weekly newspaper.*
>
> "Since a competing lower-priced newspaper, The Bugle, was started five years ago, The Mercury's circulation has declined by 10,000 readers. The best way to get more people to read The Mercury is to reduce its price below that of The Bugle, at least until circulation increases to former levels. The increased circulation of The Mercury will attract more businesses to buy advertising space in the paper."
>
> *Discuss how well reasoned you find this argument. In your discussion, be sure to analyze the line of reasoning and the use of evidence in the argument. For example, you may need to consider what questionable assumptions underlie the thinking and what alternative explanations or counterexamples might weaken the conclusion. You can also discuss what sort of evidence would strengthen or refute the argument, what changes in the argument would make it more logically sound, and what, if anything, would help you better evaluate its conclusion.*

The argument part:

(1) *"The following appeared ... a weekly newspaper"* – This part tells us from where the argument has been picked up. We can incorporate this info bit into the wording of the essay. Instead of saying "the argument states this or that" we can state "The announcement ..." or "The Mercury ...". You should be aware of where the argument has been picked from to understand its context.

(2) *"Since a competing ... by 10,000 readers"* – This is a premise, a fact, in the given argument. Based on this data, the announcement in The Mercury has made a claim.

(3) *"The best way ... increases to former levels"* - This is the primary claim or conclusion made by the announcement/argument. The validity of this is doubtful because it is based on incomplete evidence and flawed assumptions.

(4) *"The increased ... in the paper"* - This is an additional claim made by the argument/announcement. Since this claim, too, is based on the same incomplete evidence and faulty assumptions, it is also flawed and unsound.

How to actually analyze the faulty assumptions and dig out the missing evidence will be covered in the subsequent section, especially in the brainstorming part. For now, let us move on to the prompt and analyze it.

The prompt:

The prompt given for any argument remains the same. Let's analyze it sentence by sentence.

(1) *Discuss how well reasoned you find this argument.*

> This part is a general instruction telling us we have to write an essay that discusses the logic and reasoning of the given argument. So, the primary task is to pin down and cogently explain the logical flaws in the argument.

(2) *In your discussion, be sure to analyze the line of reasoning and the use of evidence in the argument.*

> This part starts by specifying what we need to particularly analyze, that is, the line of reasoning and the use of evidence. Thus, these are the two main areas we need to consider when evaluating any AWA argument.

(3) *For example, you may need to consider what questionable assumptions underlie the thinking and what alternative explanations or counterexamples might weaken the conclusion.*

> This part is very helpful and provides a clue that the AWA argument will contain faulty assumptions and that there are other possible interpretations of the given data that can weaken the conclusion made by the argument. Thus, this part establishes that all arguments given by the AWA will be weak and contains flaws.

(4) *You can also discuss what sort of evidence would strengthen or refute the argument, what changes in the argument would make it more logically sound, and what, if anything, would help you better evaluate its conclusion.*

> This part explains that after weakening the argument, the essay should suggest proper remedies to eliminate those issues, remedies such as what the author can add to make his argument less vulnerable. However, don't bring in too much outside information or construct elaborate alternative scenarios. This is a "you can also" task, and not a "you must also" task. This part does not wish to test your ability to create imaginative situations, but only to see your problem-solving capabilities and the quality of your recommendations.

Thus, we need to evaluate the argument, explain why its reasoning is faulty and its use of evidence insufficient and then explain how to deal with those issues to make the argument stronger.

The argument provided is never strong. It always contains flaws.

Let's take a look at the two basic parameters provided by the prompt: line of reasoning and use of evidence. We will analyze what they mean.

Line of reasoning

This aspect pertains to the way the argument has been constructed, that is, whether the main conclusion is based on assumptions and whether those assumptions are warranted. To analyze the line of reasoning, think of the following:

(1) Is the main conclusion based on assumptions?

(2) What are the assumptions?

(3) Are these assumptions justified?

(4) Why aren't the assumptions justified?

(5) What data could help to evaluate the assumptions? (at this point your thoughts will cross over to the "use of evidence" part)

Use of evidence

This aspect is linked to the assumptions part. The fact is that because the use of evidence is insufficient to prove the main conclusion, the conclusion is said to rely on unwarranted assumptions. Thus, for every unjustified assumption you pin down, you will find that related data is missing, and that the data needs to be incorporated to make the claim valid. Ask yourself:

(1) Is the main conclusion the only possible interpretation of the evidence?

(2) What alternative interpretations are possible?

(3) What evidence should have been given to negate the alternative interpretations?

(4) What evidence would have addressed the faulty assumptions?

(5) What could the author have provided to prove what he wishes to prove?

Note that your task is not to agree or disagree with the author. You have to critique the argument, provide its main weaknesses, and explain them. You can choose to discuss how to strengthen that claim. However, your primary concern should be the major flaws in the argument and their explanations.

How to ideate

To generate ideas to write your essay, first remember that you need ideas along a set pattern, that is,

Find a flaw

⇓

Identify its underlying assumption

⇓

Identify the relevant requisite evidence to deal with it

Sticking to this pattern will keep your thinking structured in the ideation part. Also, even if you don't adhere to the actual series, and end up achieving, say, the second or the third step (find an assumption or missing evidence), you can still find its associated flaw. Don't be finicky about how you think and in which order as long as you get the creative juices flowing.

As the first step, you should analyze the argument, sentence by sentence. A trick to understanding the argument and its flaws better is to take each sentence and rephrase it mentally. That may show you how it is meant to serve as proof. At each premise, ask yourself whether it is sufficient to prove the claim and what facts is the premise taking for granted? What else should the author have said besides that premise? What can strengthen that premise? When you reach the claim, ask yourself whether it is justified and what other information you would require.

On your scratch paper you can choose to draw a mini table of the following sort to keep track of your thoughts and later on apportion sections of it to specific body paragraphs.

Line #	Sufficient ?	Assumption ?	More proof ?	Flaw ?	Counter ?
1	N	...	...	...	...
2	N	...	...	...	...

Let's try this method on the argument.

The following appeared in an announcement issued by the publisher of The Mercury, a weekly newspaper:

"Since a competing lower-priced newspaper, The Bugle, was started five years ago, The Mercury's circulation has declined by 10,000 readers. The best way to get more people to read The Mercury is to reduce its price below that of The Bugle, at least until circulation

---

increases to former levels. The increased circulation of The Mercury will attract more businesses to buy advertising space in the paper."

Line #	Sufficient?	Assumption?	More proof?	Flaw?	Counter?
1-Premise	No	Bugle is directly responsible for reduced circulation. No other factor is responsible.	How did Bugle affect Mercury's circulation? Data on other possible factors, such as quality of Mercury, change in the market?	Assumed cause and effect for two events happening together, without providing proof	What if something else reduced Mercury's circulation?
2-Plan	No	Best way is this plan. Price is the only factor that readers of these newspapers consider. The people wouldn't switch back to Bugle after Mercury raises its price again	How the best plan? Details about other possible plans? What factors affect circulation?	Assumed plan is best Assumed plan would work Assumed plan's effect would not wear off when conditions revert	What if there are other better plans to revive circulation? What if people still don't switch to Mercury? What if people change to Bugle after Mercury raises its prices again?
3-Main claim	No	Circulation is the only significant factor in influencing advertising.	What factors determine advertising?	Assumed advertisers are swayed by circulation	What if advertisers are concerned about other things?

The line by line method will probably not yield the flaw. To understand the kind of flaws that are present, go through the commonest flaws table that follows. Study it thoroughly and learn to identify these flaws in the subsequent sample essays and the remaining AWA arguments from the pool. These flaws recur constantly. In fact, these flaws make up the flaws present in almost all the arguments.

Assumption	Faulty Assumption	Required Relevant evidence
Assumed positive correlation as cause and effect	The author assumes that both X and Y underwent changes, so X must be the cause of Y.	How is X specifically the direct cause of Y?
Assumed no alternative cause	The author assumes that only X has caused Y without considering alternative causes.	Whether there are alternative possible causes? How is only X responsible for Y?
Assumed related because of sequence	X happened before Y, or Y happened after X; therefore, X caused Y, just because they happened one after another.	How does the sequence prove that X caused Y? What are other possible factors?
Assumed representative data	The author provides sample data and assumes that it is representative.	Whether the data is representative and how specifically so?
Assumed vague terminology	The author assumes things are important by use of vague or extreme terminology.	Specific data rather than terms and generalizations
Assumed percents are significant in numbers	The author provides data in percentages and assumes that it is significant in numbers too, or provides data in numbers and assumes it is significant overall.	What is the entire picture? The data in both numbers and percentages
Assumed future based on past	The author provides past performance and assumes it would be so in the future.	How would that performance be repeated? Specifics about the plans. Past performance is only indicative, not predictive.
Assumed necessary	The author assumes that something is needed without stating why.	What should he have provided to prove it is needed?
Assumed justified	The author does not give logical reasons for why a particular thing is needed.	What reasons should he have given instead, and with what evidence?
Assumed viable	The author does not give the cost-benefit analysis/financials of the whole recommendation, or contingency plans.	Should have given specific financial plan details

Assumed compliance	The author fails to mention all stakeholders' positions, and has assumed that everyone will be okay.	He should have provided details of impact on all stakeholders and a specific plan on how to deal with/minimize the impact.
Assumed comparable	The author compares two entities without first establishing that they are comparable.	Should have specified exactly how they are comparable

3.2 How to structure the essay

The basic structure for any formal essay includes three elements:

(1) Introduction

(2) Body

(3) Conclusion

The Introduction [4 sentences, max]

(1) Sum up the argument briefly and generally. This always serves as a good anchor and ensures the elimination of writer's block. You can begin with "The argument claims that ..." Remember to just mention, without judgment, the main point and its basis. Don't end up repeating the entire argument. Use a couple of sentences at the most for this step.

(2) The next point in the introduction is to state your position in a general way. You can state that the argument is weak because it relies on a faulty line of reasoning and lack of evidence. Use a couple of sentences, if needed. Even one sentence is fine.

(3) Sum up the flaws in general. Present a sentence that briefly introduces the flaws you wish to pinpoint. You can use the flaw titles from the above table.

The Body [2-3 paragraphs]

Choose 3-5 key flaws at most and divide them up into 2-3 body paragraphs. Don't try to write all the possible flaws. Choose the big flaws and explain them well.

Body paragraph 1

(1) Use a connector to highlight transition from the intro to the first body paragraph: To begin with, to start with, the main issue is, the primary flaw is, etc.

(2) State what the author has said and you are about to attack. [1 sentence]

(3) State your position and the reason – for example, "The author's claim seems highly unlikely because ..." [1 sentence]

(4) Explain why. You have provided a reason in the previous sentence. Now spend a couple of sentences explaining with the help of an example. You can use an alternative scenario as an example. For instance, "Consider the scenario that ..." [2 sentences]

(5) Circle back to your point. Restate how the reason you provided in point 2 made the claim weak – "This possibility proves that the conclusion is vulnerable" [1 sentence]

(6) State the next flaw and repeat steps 2-5. [3 sentences]

<u>Body paragraph 2</u>

(1) Use a connector to highlight transition from first body paragraph to the second: Furthermore, Moreover, Another issue is, A secondary problem is, etc.

(2) Repeat steps 2-6, as given in the body paragraph 1, with new points.

The Conclusion [4 sentences, max]

(1) The conclusion serves to sum up the essay and to make recommendations to the author. Don't make any new points, or discuss new flaws.

(2) Recommendations – State what the author could have done to make his argument stronger and to deal with the flaws you highlighted in the two body paragraphs [2-3 sentences]

(3) Final position – Simply state in general that because the given argument contains the given flaws, it is weak and unsound.

3.3 How to polish the essay?

To improve the language of the essay and to distinguish it, you need to use appropriate and sharp vocabulary. Therefore, we have a table of vocabulary for you to use.

Instead of this	Use this
Conclusion	claim, prediction, recommendation, proposition, assertion, declaration, affirmation, contention, outcome, position, opinion, judgment, decision, culmination, conviction, belief, inference, deduction
The author states	The writer posits, claims, postulates, proposes, asserts, predicates, propounds, puts forth, declares, expresses, affirms, maintains, contends
The author suggests	The author implies, extrapolates, deduces, intimates, offers as consideration, evokes, indirectly indicates, hints, alludes, connotes, signifies
Faulty	flawed, defective, inadequate, imperfect, blemished, impaired, inaccurate
Not enough	insufficient, partial, meagre, deficient
Provide	furnish, produce, supply, equip, offer, present, reveal
Weak	vulnerable, lacking, fallible, unsupported, unjustified, unreinforced, ineffectual, irresolute, unprotected, defenseless, untenable, unviable, unconvincing, unsatisfactory, invalid, flimsy, inconclusive, feeble, unsound, undependable, unstable, not well-founded, fallacious, erroneous, specious, illogical, unreliable
Analysis	evaluation, study, dissection, estimation, interpretation, judgment, opinion, examination, investigation
Support	bolster, advocate, aid, defend, corroborate, uphold, boost, sustain, prop, shore up, substantiate, authenticate, lend credence to, verify, attest to, defend, fortify, secure, cement, supplement, reassert, underpin
Weaken	undermine, hinder, handicap, exacerbate, impair, thwart, subvert, injure, compromise, debilitate, threaten, discredit
Prove	validate, certify, confirm, authenticate, affirm, warrant, establish, demonstrate, ascertain, establish, verify, testify, evince
Analyze	inspect, scrutinize, peruse, parse through, judge, evaluate
Explain	rationalize, clarify, justify, define, explicate, illustrate, unravel, delineate, articulate
Argue against	rebut, contend, dispute, contest, challenge, controvert, negate, belie, oppose
Vague/unclear	ambiguous, equivocal, obscure, abstruse, impenetrable, incomprehensible ill-defined
Improve	amend, reconstruct, redress, overcome, ameliorate, augment, upgrade, enhance, polish, temper, refine, elevate, hone
Assume	presume, presuppose, take for granted
Emphasize	underscore, highlight, pinpoint, accentuate, stress, underline, insist, foreground, prioritize
Strengthened	cogent, conclusive, convincing, compelling, effective, potent, sound, infallible, valid

Misleading	deceptive, specious, disingenuous, dissembling, duplicitous
Evidence	grounds, data, substantiation, demonstration, manifestations

3.4 Connectors/transitions to employ in the essay

Function	Words
To make the first point	To begin with, first off, the main point is, the primary flaw is, the biggest fallacy is
To add another point	Additionally, furthermore, moreover, also, similarly, apart from this, besides this point
To give examples	For instance, say, suppose, if, consider the case that, a possible scenario is, such as, in particular, namely, particularly, specifically, including, as an illustration, as an example, illustrated with, to list, to enumerate, to detail, to specify
To conclude	To sum up, therefore, thus, as a result, consequently, in conclusion, in final consideration, hence, so
To suggest cause or effect	Because, accordingly, so, pertinently, for this purpose, for this reason, as a basis, it follows
To emphasize	Indeed, especially, most importantly, above all, chiefly, particularly, singularly, truly, in fact
To compare	Similarly, comparatively, coupled with, correspondingly, accompanied by, likewise, in a similar fashion, analogically, in like manner, analogous to, comparable to, considering similar circumstances
To contrast	However, nevertheless, nonetheless, notwithstanding, despite, in spite of, yet, conversely, instead of, on the other hand, on the contrary, rather, while this may be true
To state exceptions	Aside from, apart from, barring, besides, except, excluding, exclusive of, other than, outside of
To restate	In other words, in point, in fact, or, in essence, that is, that is to say, in short, in brief, to put it differently
To provide a sequence	at first, first of all, to begin with, in the first place, at the same time, for now, for the time being, the next step, in time, in turn, later on, meanwhile, next, then, soon, in the meantime, later, while, earlier, simultaneously, afterward, in conclusion, with this in mind, after, afterward, before, then, once, next, last, at last, at length, first, second, etc., formerly, rarely, usually, another, finally, soon, meanwhile, at the same time, for a minute, hour, day, etc., during the morning, day, week, etc., most important, ordinarily, to begin with, generally, in order to, subsequently, previously, immediately, eventually, concurrently, simultaneously
To summarize	after all, all in all, all things considered, briefly, by and large, in any case, in any event, in brief, in conclusion, on the whole, in short, in summary, in the final analysis, in the long run, to sum up, to summarize, finally
To concede	Although, at any rate, at least, still, though, even though, granted that, while it may be true, in spite of, of course

Apart from this, note that using texting language or contractions (such as can't, don't, won't) is not recommended. Try to use formal writing, but equally don't use stiff or awkward language (such as "shall, so as to").

Chapter 4

Essays

4.1 Essay 1 (City council on the arts)

The following appeared in a memorandum issued by a large city's council on the arts.

"In a recent citywide poll, fifteen percent more residents said that they watch television programs about the visual arts than was the case in a poll conducted five years ago. During these past five years, the number of people visiting our city's art museums has increased by a similar percentage. Since the corporate funding that supports public television, where most of the visual arts programs appear, is now being threatened with severe cuts, we can expect that attendance at our city's art museums will also start to decrease. Thus some of the city's funds for supporting the arts should be reallocated to public television."

Discuss how well reasoned you find this argument. In your discussion be sure to analyze the line of reasoning and the use of evidence in the argument. For example, you may need to consider what questionable assumptions underlie the thinking and what alternative explanations or counterexamples might weaken the conclusion. You can also discuss what sort of evidence would strengthen or refute the argument, what changes in the argument would make it more logically sound, and what, if anything, would help you better evaluate its conclusion.

Understand the argument

A memo by city council states that according to a poll, compared to the situation five years ago, 15% more residents watch visual arts programs. A similar increase has happened for visits to art museums, that is 15% more than it was five years ago. The argument seems to imply that these two similar increases are not coincidental but related, i.e. the increased viewership has caused the increased attendance. Further, now corporate funding for public television is facing severe cuts. Public television airs most of the visual arts programs, and thus the apparently linked event - visitors to museums — is also threatened. Therefore, the writer recommends that some of the city's funds be used for funding public television.

Faulty assumptions

- Increased viewership of visual arts on public television is responsible for increased visits to museums

- No other event led to both increased viewership of visual arts on public television and increased visits to museums

- No other means of promotion, other than visual arts programs on public television, has led to increased visits to museums

- The population of the city has not gone up significantly enough to achieve the 15% increase in either viewership or visits to museums.

- A continued increase in visitors to museums is dependent upon continued airing of visual arts programs on public television

Missing evidence

- Particulars of other means of promotion that may have led to increased visits to museums

- Details about other events that may have brought about increased viewership of visual arts on public television or increased visits to museums

- Details about change in total population

Counter-examples

- What if some other event led to both increased viewership of visual arts on TV and increased visits to museums?

- What if the museum used some other means of promotion such as ads and awareness campaigns in newspapers or on the radio, or on banners and posters?

- What if the population of the city has increased by more than 15% and, therefore, the viewership and the visits have gone up in proportion to that?

Having analyzed the argument, you should start writing the essay. Note that you need not take any position. You must evaluate the strengths and the weaknesses of the argument. While writing the essay, your mind may churn out new ideas, and if they strengthen your analysis, you should include them. There is no need to include all the points written above, however the most important ones must figure in the essay.

Sample Essay (Score 6)

In the above memorandum, city council claims that since corporate funding for public television is being threatened, some of the city's funds should be directed to help public television. The memorandum implies that public television must be supported because it airs most of the visual arts programs, which now get fifteen percent more viewership than they did earlier. Supposedly, this increased viewership is directly responsible for the fifteen percent or so increase in number of people visiting the city's art museums. A quick read of the memorandum would suggest that it is reasonable, but a deeper evaluation would show numerous flawed assumptions and a glaring lack of evidence.

The primary flaw in the argument is the multiple unjustified assumptions made by the writer of the memorandum. The biggest assumption is that the increase in viewership and increase in visitors to museums is a cause and effect relationship, with the increase in viewership being the cause and the increase in visitors to museums being the effect of said cause. A mere positive correlation does not make a cause-effect relationship. The writer has provided no justification for claiming that the increase in one led to the increase in the other, justification such as a poll conducted on the people who state that more of them visit museums now because more of them watch programs on visual arts on public TV. What is more likely is that some other event has led to increased visits to museums.

An equally deceptive assumption is that even if visual art programs on public television increased the visitors to museums, it is the only causal factor. So many other factors can affect either increased viewership of visual arts on public TV or increased visits to museums. What if the museums had employed other means of promoting themselves, such as fliers, radio announcements or posters and banners? Better exhibitions and themed displays or shows could have raised the museum's popularity, increasing the number of visits. No evidence whatsoever has been given about the museum's activities over the past five years, details that could have yielded a clue about the increased visits to museums. A similar grievous error has been made in the case of viewership of visual arts on public TV. Increased viewership of visual arts on public TV could have happened simply due to the program directors of said programs creating more interesting content and advertising the revamped shows. Such revival of the programs could have raised viewership, while not impacting the visits to museums. To make a better evaluation, the writer of the memorandum should have shared specifics about the changes in arts programs on public TV over the past five years.

In conclusion, the writer of the memorandum sees cause and effect connections in what seem like absolute coincidences. He also fails to furnish proper information about activities of the two main parties – the museum and the art programs on public TV – over the period of the five years that he discusses. Had he done so, and provided details, a better understanding of the entire situation would have emerged and a better memorandum would have been made. As it stands, the memorandum has missed the mark quite widely, leaving it considerably vulnerable to criticism.

Explanation of score 6

This essay is superbly expressed and brilliantly logical. It meets the primary criteria of a score of 6 in that it is cogent, or clear and convincing, as well as well articulated. All the points made in the response by the writer effectively analyze the major flaws in the argument and develop the essay into an integrated critique.

The argument is quite tricky because it does not present a clear causality, but rather implies such a relationship. The writer has presented an ideal introduction to his response by perfectly summing up the argument by unravelling the hidden connections one by one from the base upwards.

The body paragraphs discuss excellent flaws of the argument: faulty assumptions and lack of evidence. The points have been presented first and the writer has done a superb job of pinning them down by explaining how these assumptions make the argument vulnerable. The quality of logic in discussing the flaws is superlative. The argument has not dwelled on any single trivial points. Minor points have been mentioned in a small but adequate way, that is, as minor points. There is no needless repetition of points or similar flaws. All of this shows a deep understanding of the way the logic of arguments works.

The arrangement and organization of the argument and its distinctive top down process of points – from general to specific and back again to general – demonstrates exceptional facility with the written language.

The use of language is extremely persuasive and the critique is completely convincing. Overall, despite lack of sentence variety, the strength of the points and neat and engaging organization makes the response outstanding.

Sample Essay (Score 5)

The Council of the Arts would like to use city funding to support public television because it fears that cuts in corporate funding of public television would adversely affect visual arts programs. The argument believes that these programs on visual arts on public television are a key factor in drawing citizens to art museums. However, this argument is undermined by two main reasons – faulty assumption that the two increased percentages are related and that no other means of promotion were used by the museum.

To start with, the argument takes for granted that increased viewing of the visual arts on television, mainly public television, has caused an analogous increase in visitors to museums. Yet, just because increased visitors to museums can be numerically correlated with increases in television exposure of visual arts programs does not necessarily suggest that the increased viewing of arts through TV is the cause of the increase in visitors to museums. The rise in viewership as well as in number of visitors should not be seen as anything but independent happenings, related only by them coincidentally being 15 percent.

Another big flaw in the argument is that it believes television to be a driving force in citizens' interest in the arts. The reasons for the growth could be several: for increased viewership, a natural population growth curve, more compelling production and visual features, etc.; for increased visitors, increased attendance by schools and colleges, more tourists to the city, etc. Such connections fail to take into account other mass media that the museum may have used to generate interest in art among citizens. Radio, newspapers, and magazines, too, can be put to use to encourage art awareness. If the museum curator has acquired some interesting exhibitions and pieces, as well as publicized them, visitors to museums can increase. Also, charity events with influential visitors and celebrities, too, can be organized by city officials or the museum itself to encourage visitors. All these measures can significantly boost interest and thus visits to art institutions. However, the argument does not mention these possible alternatives or lack thereof. If the argument had mentioned to what extent the television programs on visual arts contribute to increased visitors to museums, the argument would be more justified.

Reasonably, however, we must acknowledge that the assumption in the argument is a one-off case of a more general nature: TV viewing influences people's behavior and inclinations. Practical knowledge and empirical data tell me that this is indeed the situation in real life. This assumption is exactly why the advertising business is a trillion-dollar industry. However, it is not acceptable to use this generalization to make financial decisions.

To conclude, I am only partly convinced by this argument's line of reasoning. The argument would be stronger if it had considered other significant factors that might have caused the increase in art visitors to museums. Finally, to simply say that because corporate funding (which supports public television) is likely to decrease, one should divert the city's funds to public television is equally invalid in the absence of a clear and definite correlation between the two – television viewership and patronage of art museums.

Explanation of score 5

This response strongly presents a good critique of the given argument. It starts with a comprehensive introduction of the argument that highlights its main flaws.
In the body, the two main paragraphs present the two big flaws of the argument - the possibility of a positive numerical relation between two numbers not necessarily being a cause and effect relationship, and failing to consider promotion options other than the television. Both these points have been presented in a coherent manner by first stating the point and then explaining why the points are construed as flaws and supporting them with relevant examples. The logic that has been employed is presented sensibly.

Logical organization of the argument has not left anything lacking. There are clear and sensible supporters and connectors throughout the argument. The writer presents a well-developed critique of the argument and demonstrates good control of the elements of effective writing.

Even in the conclusion of the argument, the writer makes a good point that generalizations are generally true, but not a sound basis for decisions. However, the response cannot earn higher than a score of 5 because there are important points missing, points such as use of vague terminology by the memorandum writer and hardly any syntactical variety – just a few "if" sentences. Also, the use of the word "the argument" instead of "memorandum" shows lack of awareness to some extent.

The essay demonstrates ease with the conventions of standard written English. The critique raises valid points and develops them sensibly.

Sample Essay (Score 4)

This argument concludes that the city council should allocate some of its arts funding to public television. The conclusion is based on two premises: (1) attendance at the city's art museums has increased proportionally with the increases in visual arts program viewing on public television compared to five years ago, and (2) public television is going to face severe cuts from corporate funding. While this argument is somewhat convincing, a few concerns need to be addressed.

The main problem is the argument's assumption that attendance at the city's art museums has increased proportionally because of visual arts program viewing on public television. It is likely that there are other aspects connected to increased attendance at museums. For example, maybe a new curator could have acquired more interesting, exciting exhibition pieces for the period when visitors to museums rose. Additionally, the argument does not consider any common cause of both increases. Probably there are some community, social or cultural programs or festivals that are responsible for greater numbers in both television arts viewing and art visitors to museums.

Furthermore, cuts in television spending could boost other leisure and entertainment options for citizens - one of them being art museums themselves. Citizens would begin looking at various other ways and places to relax and spend time together with family. Art museums provide for a fun group activity. Thus, a disinterest in television could drive citizens to art museums.

Lastly, redirecting funds meant to support arts would adversely affect artists. Creativity requires the necessary funding for support. Artists who do not have wealthy patrons, especially up and coming ones, would not be able to make a living without the support of funds from the Council of the Arts. Thus in order to drive traffic to museums, the council would be compromising on the art itself.

In sum, the above argument fails to consider these key factors and their effects. If the funding were to be redirected, it should be limited and channelled only towards art shows. Therefore, more analysis is required before making a decision in this matter.

Explanation of Score 4

This response cites a number of deficiencies in the argument presented in an adequate manner: other possible media of promotion, alternative interpretation of given actions, etc.

Although the points cited in the argument are well-arranged and presented in an understandable manner, the quality of the points is inconsistent. Only the first main point is a logically acceptable point of good quality – that there could be other means of promotion by which the attendance at the museums has increased. The other two points are not important enough to warrant stand-alone paragraphs. While the general idea behind them is legitimate, the examples used are quite implausible and are more in the nature of absurd exceptions rather than a general possibility. These points weaken the response overall and take the focus away from the main flaws of the argument. Several other key points from the argument could have been picked: lack of proof that the increase in television art program viewing is connected to the increased visits to museums, use of vague terms such as "some funds", etc. While the other points are not illegitimate, they are not logically on par with the point in the first paragraph.

The presentation of ideas, while generally adequate, is sometimes weakened by lack of full development of certain points. For example, both the second and third paragraphs in the body could have been explained and developed better and such development might have taken the attention away from the poor quality of logic involved in these paragraphs.

Further, the writing contains minor examples of awkwardness, but is free of flaws generally. Only a few sentences begin with "if" clauses, but almost all the rest, even those that begin with a transitional phrase such as "for example" or "in addition," stick to a standard pattern. Overall, uninspiring but adequate.

Sample Essay (Score 2)

To begin with, the author correlated similar increase in the viewership of art related television programs and the increase in museum visitation hastily without presenting all the facts. Consider a possibility that that may impact the above premise are introduction of compulsory arts class in all schools by school boards and strong promotion of museum visitation as relaxing break to the population. Education law was passed five years back mandating visitation to museum as a part of graded curriculum by every student to promote arts which result in increases visitations. Such external factors are not provided by the author in the argument. Other examples of external factors.

In conclusion, the author provides facts and argument with mistakes that leaves much to be desired. The lack of all the relevant facts, faulty line of reasoning and hasty conclusion of the argument does not work well. Author should substantiate the argument with more relevant details and provide readers with logical reasoning and conclusion.

Explanation of Score 2

This response is quite deficient in many ways.

The biggest problem is the lack of material provided in it. The writer has made one point only throughout the essay. The point itself is extremely weak in logic: an education law or compulsory art classes can hardly account for the situation given in the argument. While this example could have worked as a subsidiary minor point, to present it as the main and the only flaw in an argument that has far more serious flaws is completely unacceptable.

Even if the poor quality of logic is ignored, the organization of the essay leaves much to be desired. There is no functional introduction to the argument, because the writer has started his attack within a couple of sentences of beginning his essay response. Overall, there are no transitions given clearly enough. There is virtually no demarcation from point to example. In fact, the example is supposed to serve as the point. The point, furthermore, is neither explained by a single reason beyond what is given in the topic. It is not an incorrect point, but alone and undeveloped, it cannot serve as an adequate response to the argument.

The general lack of coherence is reflected in the serious and frequent writing problems that make meaning hard to determine—for example, the last couple of sentence of the first paragraph are fragments and probably meant to serve as a hypothetical example, but are clearly neither here nor there.

4.2 Essay 2 (Violence in movies)

> *The following appeared in a newspaper editorial.*
>
> "As violence in movies increases, so do crime rates in our cities. To combat this problem we must establish a board to censor certain movies, or we must limit admission to persons over 21 years of age. Apparently our legislators are not concerned about this issue since a bill calling for such actions recently failed to receive a majority vote."
>
> *Discuss how well reasoned you find this argument. In your discussion be sure to analyze the line of reasoning and the use of evidence in the argument. For example, you may need to consider what questionable assumptions underlie the thinking and what alternative explanations or counterexamples might weaken the conclusion. You can also discuss what sort of evidence would strengthen or refute the argument, what changes in the argument would make it more logically sound, and what, if anything, would help you better evaluate its conclusion.*

Understand the argument

A newspaper editor states that rising crime is related to the violence shown in movies. He recommends following one of two courses of actions: 1) establish a censor board or 2) limit admission to such movies to only those over the age of 21. His opinion of legislators and the matter is that they do not care about the issue because it failed to get a majority vote.

Faulty assumptions

- Increased violence in movies is responsible for increased crime rates in the cities

- Nothing else has led to increased crime rates in the cities

- People over 21 years of age will not be influenced to commit crimes after watching the increased violence in movies. People under 21 years of age will not watch those censored movies through some other media such as television or the internet

- Passing a bill about a censor board with a clear majority is the sole way legislators can demonstrate concern for the issue

Missing evidence

- Proof that increased crime rates in the cities is caused by increased violence in movies

- Proof that persons over 21 years of age will not be influenced to commit crimes

- Proof that limiting admission to persons over 21 years of age will ensure that no persons under 21 years of age watch those censored movies through some other medium

- Details about other factors that can affect crime rates, such as the state of the economy

- Details about the demographics involved in criminal activities

- Details about the law and order situation in the cities

· Details about legislation, passed or under discussion, pertaining to crimes and related laws

Counter-examples

· What if some other event led to increased crime rates in the cities, events such as increased unemployment, failure of law and order machinery, etc?

· What if some other bill to better law and order has been passed by legislators with a clear majority?

· What if the crime rates show that most of the crimes are committed by people over 21 years of age?

· What if persons under 21 years of age watch those censored movies through some other media such as television or the internet?

· What if the movies, portraying reality, are showing increased violence because the cities have increased crime rates?

Having analyzed the argument, you should start writing the essay. Note that you need not take any position. You must evaluate the strengths and the weaknesses of the argument. While writing the essay, your mind may churn out new ideas. If they strengthen your analysis, you should include them. There is no need to include all the points written above, however the most important ones must figure in the essay.

Sample Essay (Score 6)

In the given editorial, the editor claims that because violence in the movies is increasing, crime in cities is increasing. According to the editor, the corrective measure for this situation is establishing a censor board to prevent the entry of persons under 21 years of age to such movies. He also claims that legislators are not concerned about increasing crime rates because they did not pass a bill on such a board a with majority vote. The editorial has a long way to go to be considered convincing because it is riddled with unsubstantiated assumptions and a lack of understanding of important issues.

Primarily, the editor seems to have completely misunderstood the situation at hand. He states that increasing crime rates can be directly attributed to increasing violence in the movies. Even if we were to suspend judgment on this obviously flawed connection here, the editor has not provided an iota of proof for claiming this connection. Apart from the fact that two things are increasing, there's no other evidence provided to claim that increase in one of those two things is the cause of the increase in the other. The editor has taken a complex issue - increasing crime rate - and applied a simplistic analysis on it, making the whole issue seem ludicrous. An increasing crime rate can be an outcome of multiple issues, issues such as low employment rates, class differences, inadequate machinery of law and order, poor functioning of the economy, political instability, etc. It is quite likely that because the crime rate is increasing, that to portray reality, the violence in movies is increasing. To even assume the reverse is absurd.

Aside from the editor's lack of understanding of increasing crime rates, another major fallacy is his understanding of crimes and criminals. His proposition that entry to certain violent movies should be restricted to persons over 21 years of age implies two extraordinary things – that only persons under 21 years of age commit crimes or that only persons under 21 years of age get influenced to commit crimes by the violent content in movies. For argument's sake, let's assume that this assumption is not incorrect. What about the innumerable other ways that a person under 21 years of age can use to lay his hands on such movies, if he were so inclined to? Maybe the editor assumes that the next step in reducing crime would be to censor and restrict the internet! The editor needs to understand that crime is not necessarily age-specific and depends on a lot of factors, such as social situations, associated risks, possibility of being caught, etc. Not every person under 21 years of age is prone to becoming a criminal nor is every person over it immune from the same.

Finally, the author blames legislators for being unconcerned about the increasing crime rate, as demonstrated by their not passing a bill by majority vote, a bill on establishing a sort of censor board. There are numerous reasons a bill can get rejected, the least of which is lack of concern with an issue. The legislators could have thought the wording of the bill ambiguous or not strong enough. Probably, the legislators know that increasing crime rates is a composite issue that needs a many-pronged approach and decided to pursue a variety of redressal mechanisms such as tightening law and order, working on the causes of the increasing crime rate, etc.

To conclude, the editorial is so poorly constructed that finding any redeeming qualities is difficult. However, had the author noted the discussed points and added proof for every claim, the editorial would have been far more sound than it is now.

Explanation of score 6

This response is cogent, sharp, and extremely well-articulated.

The introduction comprehensively covers all the aspects of the editorial and in a direct manner states that the editorial is flawed. The body covers all the possible flaws of the editorial – faulty assumption that increasing violence in movies is responsible for the increasing crime rate, and that persons under 21 years of age are susceptible to committing crimes or being influenced by violence in the movies, as well as the editor's lack of understanding of important issues.

The first body paragraph tackles the faulty assumption that increasing violence in movies is responsible for the increasing crime rate. The response brilliantly strips away the lack of proof or connection in the flawed assumption and correctly analyzes that two positively correlated things are not necessarily in a cause and effect relationship. The writer also displays a nuanced understanding of crime and provides a well-supported point that crime is a composite issue. The points in the response are completely substantiated by alternative reasoning.

In the second body paragraph, the writer discusses the fallacy that persons under 21 years of age are susceptible to committing crimes or being influenced by violence in the movies. The point has been made using syntactical variety with incisive logical analysis. Also, a linked issue has been addressed in this paragraph that even if entry of persons under 21 years of age were restricted, they would be able to watch the movies in some way or the other.

In the final body paragraph, the writer explains in a succinct way how the apparent situation with legislators has been misinterpreted. The conclusion is short and pithy and not repetitive.

It crisply concludes the brilliant response.

The use of language is persuasive and forceful. The variety of syntax – rhetorical questions, if clauses, etc, makes the response fresh and keeps it from becoming tedious. The quality of logic is consistently high.

Overall – up to the mark in all aspects.

Sample Essay (Score 5)

In this argument, the author seeks to establish a correlation between violence in movies and crime rates in cities. The author suggests that a board be established to censor movies with violent content or limit admission to adolescents under 21 years of age. Also, he has generalized a point that legislators are nonchalant about the problem of crime rate in cities. The argument on the whole is unconvincing as it is devoid of convincing evidence and assumes the conclusion it should have proved.

To start with, the very premise of the argument is flawed because the author has assumed that increased violence in movies is responsible for increased crime in cities. A mere positive correlation between increased violence in movies and increased crime in cities cannot be translated into a causal relationship. That the author has failed to provide any strong or direct evidence or illustration of his point leaves the argument unsubstantiated. This lack leads to a slippery assumption that crime in movies is always glorified and influences adolescents in the formative years of their adulthood. The author has not taken into consideration any other factors such as people's general predisposition towards violence, the class divide, unemployment, poverty and other prevalent illegal activities in a city. Ignoring possible causative factors while honing in on a single and possibly unrelated factor makes the argument highly vulnerable to criticism. Further, the author seems not to have addressed some examples that would negate the point he has made. For example, so-called violent movies made by renowned movie-makers such as Martin Scorsese and Quentin Tarantino have cut across all age groups, genders, and races to win critical acclaim. The violence content in their movies may appear grotesque to some, yet there haven't been any reported surges in violence after the release of their movies. Crimes have been prevalent even in eras before movies existed.

Another shaky point made in the argument is that adolescents or teenagers are adversely affected by violence in movies. This implies that the perpetrators of crime in cities are mostly juveniles and that people above the age of 21 aren't as susceptible to committing crimes. However, no statistics or examples have been presented towards the same.

In all, the legislators did not rely on oversimplified solutions put forth by the author. Their lack of support for the proposed alternatives does not reflect their lack of concern for crime rates in cities. Instead, they did not opt for a generic solution for a problem that is seemingly more complex. Crime is a product of myriad factors. As there is a lack of evidence or examples to bolster the author's viewpoint, the author's solution does not really elicit a lot of conviction. To make it more convincing, the author must address the issues discussed above and support his points with thorough evidence.

Explanation of score 5

The response contains organized discussion of legitimate flaws in a sensible manner with good examples. However, not all logical flaws have been discussed in the argument.

The introduction of the essay is good but lacking in certain aspects: it mentions all the details from the argument but does not link them in the correct relationship as given in the argument. For example, the editor of the editorial implies that because legislators did not pass legislation regarding a bill on establishing a censor board, legislators are not concerned about the issue.

In the first body paragraph, the writer raises a valid and strong point about the unsubstantiated claim made by the editor in his editorial. The faulty assumption of the editor is that increased violence in movies is responsible for increased crime in cities. The evaluation part of this assumption is thoroughly developed by the writer and neatly explained. Good examples have been provided by the writer, examples that weaken the editor's case. However, too much emphasis has been given to just this one point. The writer could have taken up a more detailed discussion of what can lead to increased crime in cities, or of the fact that increased violence in movies is merely a reflection of the reality that crime in cities has increased.

In the second body paragraph, the writer raises another legitimate point about the flimsy claim made by the editor in his editorial. The flawed assumption of the editor is that only people below 21 years of age are susceptible to the influence of violence in movies. The point is developed sensibly. If the writer had discussed some more points here, such as the faulty assumptions of the editor regarding the legislators, this response would have been strengthened.

The conclusion is well-stated and includes some of the points that should have been touched upon in the body, thus redeeming the essay. The use of language is persuasive but not forceful enough. The quality of logic is strong, but lacks consistency to a minor extent. The grasp on standards of English is strong and convincing.

Overall – a sensible, strong and convincing response.

Sample Essay (Score 4)

In the above argument, the author states that the as violence in movies increases, so do crime rates. To combat this problem he suggests that a censor board must be established or admission be reserved to persons over 21 years of age. It also states that the legislators are not concerned about this issue since a bill calling for such actions recently failed to receive a majority vote. At first, these factors in the argument look connected however on closer evaluation there seem to be several flaws.

To begin with, the author states that as violence in movies increases, so do crime rates. This conclusion seems a little hasty as the author does not provide any substantial evidence. The author also does not provide any particular time frame for this. For example, there could have been a government change or political instability which might be the reason for the rise in crime rates. Thus, if the author had provided statistics linking the violence in movies with the rise in crime rates, his argument would have been stronger.

Further, the author says that a censor board must be established or admission be reserved to persons over 21 years of age. While the censor board will be able to curtail the content that is shown in the movies ,there is a flaw with the reservation on admissions. Consider the case in which recent rises in crime rates have been because of adults above the age of 30. In that case, reserving admission to persons over 21 years of age will be of no help. Had the author provided sufficient data highlighting how the recent rise in crime rates was due to persons under the age of 21, the argument could have been stronger.

Also, the author then goes on to say that legislators are not concerned about this issue because a bill calling for such actions recently failed to receive a majority vote. This again seems like a hasty conclusion on the author's part. If the author provided information on the merits and the demerits of the bill, his argument could have been stronger.

In conclusion, the author furnishes several bits of data without providing sufficient statistics. This makes his argument weak. Had the author provided statistics or more information on the data provided, his arguments could have been stronger.

Explanation of (Score 4)

The above response is adequate – logical enough but lacks strong examples and forceful use of language.

The introduction is clear and well-written but not brilliant enough to introduce the flaws. It includes nothing more than a summary of the editorial and a general statement about the flaws with no details. Suitable but not superb.

The flaws discussed in all the body paragraphs are strong fallacies of the editorial: lack of proof of the faulty claim that increased violence in movies is responsible for increased crime in cities and that only people under 21 years of age are influenced by violence in the movies, or that crime is not committed by anyone over 21 years of age. While the logic itself is sound, very little explanation of why the assumptions are wrong is given. The examples used to illustrate the problem in the editorial are not reasonable, and are rather difficult to believe. In fact, only the first body paragraph has an example to support its point, but the next two paragraphs lack any explanation or examples. Thus, the critique is not well-supported.

The organization of the essay is neat enough with clear demarcations for the introduction, the body and the conclusion. However, there is very little sentence variety. All the sentences are simple and similar in structure. The use of "argument would have been stronger" or "hasty conclusion" is a bit repetitive.

Overall, adequate but not very strong or persuasive.

Sample Essay score 2

The above argument states that violence in movie increases along with the crime rate in the city. The editor then conclude that there must be censor on certain movies and there should be restriction over admission of more than 21 year of adult to watch the movie. On initial evaluation the argument seem convincing, but a more detailed analysis reveals certain flaws.

The most overt flaws in the argument are unsubstantiated assumptions and a hasty conclusion.

Firstly, the newspaper editor states that violence and crime have increase in city and to overcome this issue there should be censor on certain move and age restriction should be present in order to avoid crime. This seems a bit ambiguous. Also consider that legislator are not concerned about crimes and the bill which was initiated failed due to less majority votes because there was less preferment done on this bill . Crime may have happened if there is any person who is mentally ill and who just want to take revenge to eradicate people.

Author should have consider various factors before coming to any conclusion regarding crimes, along with that there is no clear wordings that legislator were actually concern regarding the Bill which got failed due to majority of voting.

In conclusion, the argument is improper for assuming censor on violated movies and age limit for certain movie will reduce the crime rates, also the bill failed due to less votes received. Editor should look at the broad picture before any conclusion and consider various fact.

Explanation of score 2

The above response is inadequate – severely flawed with many errors in grammar.

The introduction seems reasonable enough but the rest of the essay is just filled with errors. The logic is difficult to decipher. One cannot make out clearly enough the point being made in any of the body paragraphs. Also, the logic seems inconsistent. While the writer starts with criticizing the editor, the final body paragraph seems to be supporting the editor's point. Examples seem completely ludicrous. The writer seems to suggest that crime rates can go up because of the mentally ill and people who want to get revenge! The logic cannot be evaluated further because the erroneous language hampers the understanding of the essay.

The various subject-complement agreement errors break the flow of the argument and are too conspicuous to be mere typos. For example, "editor then conclude" and "violence and crime have increase", etc. The entire essay demonstrates that the writer has no control of the basics of the language and is unaware of the devices of grammar.

Overall, completely flawed with absurd indecipherable reasoning.

4.3   Essay 3 (The Bugle newspaper)

The following appeared in an announcement issued by the publisher of The Mercury, a weekly newspaper.

"Since a competing lower-priced newspaper, The Bugle, was started five years ago, The Mercury's circulation has declined by 10,000 readers. The best way to get more people to read The Mercury is to reduce its price below that of The Bugle, at least until circulation increases to former levels. The increased circulation of The Mercury will attract more businesses to buy advertising space in the paper."

Discuss how well reasoned you find this argument. In your discussion be sure to analyze the line of reasoning and the use of evidence in the argument. For example, you may need to consider what questionable assumptions underlie the thinking and what alternative explanations or counterexamples might weaken the conclusion. You can also discuss what sort of evidence would strengthen or refute the argument, what changes in the argument would make it more logically sound, and what, if anything, would help you better evaluate its conclusion.

Understand the argument

The publisher announced that The Mercury's circulation started declining upon The Bugle's entry and has now declined by 10,000 readers. The publisher implies that the circulation has dropped because The Bugle is a lower-priced newspaper. The publisher is planning to reduce the price of The Mercury to make it cheaper than The Bugle. This move, according to the publisher, would not only increase circulation, but also fetch advertisers.

Faulty assumptions

- No other reason for decline of The Mercury's circulation

- Only lowering the price would be enough to lure readers back to The Mercury

- The Bugle wouldn't also lower its price to retain its customers

- A newspaper's circulation is the only factor that the advertisers look at

- Raising prices later would not cause circulation to decline again

Missing evidence

- The Bugle is directly responsible for reducing The Mercury's circulation by 10,000 readers

- Proof that readers are only concerned about a newspaper's price and the advertisers are only concerned about a newspaper's circulation

- The situation of the market, whether the public is interested in newspapers

- Proof that The Mercury itself did not lose its circulation through some fault of its own

Counter-examples

- What if The Mercury's quality has declined, causing the readers to switch to The Bugle?

- What if some other newspaper has snatched the readers from The Mercury?

- What if people are no longer interested in newspapers and have moved to digital media?

- What if cutting prices starts price wars that cause deep losses and are impossible to sustain?

- Even if the plan is successful, when The Mercury raises its price, wouldn't the circulation drop and advertisers leave?

Having analyzed the argument, you should start writing the essay. Note that you need not take any position. You must evaluate the strengths and the weaknesses of the argument. While writing the essay, your mind may churn out new ideas. If they strengthen your analysis, you should include them. There is no need to include all the points written above, however the most important ones must figure in the essay.

The essay

The publisher of the Mercury has implied in an announcement that The Bugle, a competing newspaper, is responsible for reducing The Mercury's circulation by being lower-priced. It concludes that The Mercury should reduce its price to increase circulation while simultaneously attracting more advertisers. The argument is flawed in not considering alternative causes of the current situation, thereby relying on simplistic, incorrect assumptions.

To begin with, to state that The Mercury's circulation declined by 10,000 readers over a five-year period only since a lower-priced competitor showed up is to assume that a newspaper's circulation depends only on the pricing. This view is oversimplified and illogical because it does not take into consideration other factors that may have affected The Mercury's circulation. Problems within The Mercury itself could have reduced its circulation; problems such as sliding quality, production issues, etc.; thus blaming The Bugle alone for declining circulation is incorrect. In fact, it hasn't even been established that the 10,000 readers that have moved away from The Mercury have switched to the Bugle! It is possible that the circulation has declined because the readers have moved to digital media, leaving both The Mercury and The Bugle, and any other newspaper, suffering reduced circulation. In light of these multiple possibilities, taking a myopic view is completely illogical.

Even if one were to accept the assumption that the lower price of its competitor is responsible for the reduced circulation of The Mercury, it would be unreasonable to assume that merely reducing its own price lower than The Bugle would attract both readers and advertisers. Assuming that people's and advertisers' sentiments are easily swayed, what if The Bugle, along with the other newspapers, if any, launches a price war? Merely reducing prices to attract more business can easily backfire because such a move needs potentially deep coffers and a lot of patience, five years at least as per the announcement. Also, simply cutting prices without determining whether it is sustainable over the long-term is fraught with risk. The publisher is also suspiciously quiet about how The Mercury would plan to keep the readers and the advertisers after having lured them with reduced prices.

What the publisher should do instead is analyze why the circulation has dropped, whether cost of production can be cut, and what alternative measures can increase The Mercury's circulation. Jumping on a "me-too" bandwagon seldom works well. Had the publisher considered the various aspects discussed above, the argument would have been far more convincing than it is at present.

4.4 Essay 4 (Apogee Company)

> *The following appeared in a memorandum from the business department of the Apogee Company.*
>
> "When the Apogee Company had all its operations in one location, it was more profitable than it is today. Therefore, the Apogee Company should close down its field offices and conduct all its operations from a single location. Such centralization would improve profitability by cutting costs and helping the company maintain better supervision of all employees."
>
> *Discuss how well reasoned you find this argument. In your discussion be sure to analyze the line of reasoning and the use of evidence in the argument. For example, you may need to consider what questionable assumptions underlie the thinking and what alternative explanations or counterexamples might weaken the conclusion. You can also discuss what sort of evidence would strengthen or refute the argument, what changes in the argument would make it more logically sound, and what, if anything, would help you better evaluate its conclusion.*

Understand the argument

A memo by the business department of the Apogee Company suggests that the company should close all its field offices and become centralized, as it used to be. This move would improve profitability and supervision of all employees.

Faulty assumptions

- Field offices are no longer needed for the purpose they were created

- Closing field offices would not hamper the business

- Centralization today would be just as profitable it was earlier

- Operating with field offices in place cannot be profitable

Missing evidence

- Why aren't field offices required any longer? What use did they serve earlier and is that need not present any longer?

- Other factors related to the field offices – business connections, transactions, etc

- Reasons for lack of profitability of field offices

- Impact on all the stakeholders in this move of closing all field offices

Counter-examples

- What if clients or customers switch to some competitor that has field offices?

- What if Apogee isn't as profitable as it used to be even if it becomes centralized?

- What if the profitability of Apogee working with the field offices arrangement can be improved?

- What if the public image of the company gets spoiled by the abrupt closing of field offices, affecting business?

Having analyzed the argument, you should start writing the essay. Note that you need not take any position. You must evaluate the strengths and the weaknesses of the argument. While writing the essay, your mind may churn out new ideas. If they strengthen your analysis, you should include them. There is no need to include all the points written above, however the most important ones must figure out in the essay.

The essay

The business department of the Apogee Company suggests reverting to an earlier centralized state to improve the company's profitability. While the claim seems legitimate, it could have been improved were it not for erroneous assumptions and lack of substantiation.

To begin with, the memorandum says that the company's profitability would increase were it to shut down all its field offices. Without knowing the nature of the company's business, as well as its earlier need for field offices, a decision to do so sounds hasty and ill-planned. That Apogee has field offices implies that the company needed those offices at some point for whatever reasons. Is that need no longer applicable? Even if so, since the offices have been constructed, they must be conducting some business. How would those operations be affected by centralization? The argument suffers greatly for not providing details about how the stakeholders would be affected or what measures would be taken to minimize that impact. Another faulty line of reasoning is the business department's assumption that since it once operated out of a single location, it should now close down all its field offices. As conditions change, what served the purpose earlier may not necessarily be true at a later date. Even if one were to grant that Apogee would benefit from centralization simply because it once was so, the absence of context about changed times - and data to justify such a move - makes it impossible to accept the claim. Finally, the argument suffers from a lack of perspective of time. New field offices typically need time to function independently, come of age, and generate profits. Whether sufficient time has been given to the field offices to become as profitable as expected is not stated in the memorandum.

What the business department should do instead is thoroughly analyze the factors that made Apogee more profitable back in its earlier days and the reason that Apogee is not profitable while operating with field offices. Perhaps a halfway solution of closing some field offices while keeping some others open may work better all around. To the memorandum's argument that centralization would help in the supervision of employees, perhaps better HR policies need to be instituted and managers employed, rather than the drastic step of closing down all its field offices.

To judge whether centralization would be a better option currently, detailed evidence as discussed above needs to be provided. It is incorrect to merely compare two points of existence in a company's history and state that one particular situation is better than the other based on a single factor, especially since other factors are left unaddressed. Thus, while it probably makes a valid point, the argument is glaringly deficient.

4.5 Essay 5 (Motorcycle X)

The following appeared as part of an article in the business section of a local newspaper.

Motorcycle X has been manufactured in the United States for over 70 years. Although one foreign company has copied the motorcycle and is selling it for less, the company has failed to attract motorcycle X customers - some say because its product lacks the exceptionally loud noise made by motorcycle X. But there must be some other explanation. After all, foreign cars tend to be quieter than similar American-made cars, but they sell at least as well. Also, television advertisements for motorcycle X highlight its durability and sleek lines, not its noisiness, and the ads typically have voice-overs or rock music rather than engine roar on the sound track.

Discuss how well reasoned you find this argument. In your discussion be sure to analyze the line of reasoning and the use of evidence in the argument. For example, you may need to consider what questionable assumptions underlie the thinking and what alternative explanations or counterexamples might weaken the conclusion. You can also discuss what sort of evidence would strengthen or refute the argument, what changes in the argument would make it more logically sound, and what, if anything, would help you better evaluate its conclusion.

Understand the argument

A case has been presented about a motorcycle and its copy. Motorcycle X has been around for 70 years, and supposedly a foreign company has come to the US, copied motorcycle X and tried to sell it at a lower price to motorcycle X customers themselves. It hasn't been able to sell well to motorcycle X customers. Some feel that the copy didn't sell well to motorcycle X customers because it lacks the exceptionally loud noise made by motorcycle X. The author feels that the noise is not the reason. To make that point he gives an example of foreign cars that are copies of American-made cars but are quieter, yet sell as well as the originals. Another point the author uses to state that the noise is not the reason is that the ads of motorcycle X don't highlight noise, but play voice-overs or rock music.

Faulty assumptions

- Motorcycle X customers are willing to buy a quieter copy of motorcycle X
- Motorcycles are comparable to cars
- People buy quieter cars so people would also want to buy quieter motorcycles
- Ads don't show noise so people do not buy because of noise

Missing evidence

- Evidence that the foreign company indeed did try to copy motorcycle X and woo its customers: the foreign company's sales figures, current market position, etc
- Proof that motorcycles and cars can be compared in the quietness or noisiness aspect

· Proof that ads represent buyer behavior

Counter-examples

· What if the company only coincidentally seemed to copy motorcycle X, but isn't actually copying X, and is merely selling a similar motorcycle independently?

· What if motorcycle x customers don't buy the copy but an independent market segment does?

· People who buys cars have different reasons from people who buy motorcycles

· Ads reflect makers' intentions or product placement by marketing department but not necessarily the reason customers buy a particular product

· Just because people buy quieter cars does not mean they buy it because they want quietness; there are many other factors to consider, such as mileage, comfort, safety, etc

Having analyzed the argument, you should start writing the essay. Note that you need not take any position. You must evaluate the strengths and the weaknesses of the argument. While writing the essay, your mind may churn out new ideas. If they strengthen your analysis, you should include them. There is no need to include all the points written above, however the most important ones must figure in the essay.

The essay

In the given argument, the author seems primarily concerned with negating a specific opinion about the reason motorcycle X's copy does not sell as well as motorcycle X to motorcycle X customers. The opinion in question is that there are fewer sales by the competitor to those particular customers because the copy lacks the attribute of making an exceptionally loud noise, as is the case with motorcycle X. However, the author believes that this reason is incorrect. To support his claim, the author compares car copies to motorcycle X's copy and brings up ads of motorcycle X. The argument seems legitimate initially, but crumbles entirely upon deeper analysis.

The most profound problem with the argument is that its primary point itself seems like a moot discussion. The idea that a company has gone to the lengths of imitating an established brand to attract the existing or potential customers is difficult to accept. What is more likely is that the foreign company wishes to establish a parallel market based on the success of motorcycle X. To say that it failed to attract motorcycle X customers is to make an incorrect connection because it is quite likely that the foreign company never wanted motorcycle X customers. Maybe it wanted to get those people who would want something like motorcycle X but would be unwilling to, either due to the noise or the price, actually buy motorcycle X itself. What the author should discuss is the existing sales of the foreign company to enable analysis of its target market, and the extent of the success of its stint in America. Maybe if we delve deeply enough into the sale of the so-called copy of motorcycle X, we'll find that it has its own target market and never meant to attract motorcycle X customers. This might also imply that it never intended to copy motorcycle X. That it seems very similar to motorcycle X might just be a coincidence! Otherwise, the alternative suggestion is the author's bizarre connection that a foreign company comes to the USA, knowing very well that motorcycle X has a loyal following, given that it has been around for seventy years, but still decides to copy motorcycle X. It then attempts to lure its customers and fails in that endeavor because those customers prefer motorcycle X. Without proper details about why the foreign company copied motorcycle X and whether it has an independent market, it is impossible to evaluate the situation.

Additional problems are the multiple flawed assumptions that the author has made. The author has simply assumed that not only are cars comparable to motorcycles, but also that copies of cars are comparable to copies of motorcycles, especially when it comes to determining the market's perception of these products. The author's primary support in his statement that lack of noise is not the reason the imitator is not selling motorcycles is that foreign cars are quieter but generate as many sales as do the originals. The author has taken for granted that car buyers think like motorcycle buyers, and erroneously equates the perception of the target markets of both. However, car buyers will obviously look for characteristics different from those of motorcycle buyers. Notwithstanding the specific needs of each buyer, car buyers are likely to be concerned with comfort, safety, and luxury, while motorcycle buyers look for power, mileage, and overall performance. Furthermore, just because cars that are quieter have better sales does not necessarily mean that they sell because they are quieter. Likewise, the sales of the imitator of motorcycle X may very well have nothing to do with the noise factor. Merely providing two sets of positively related data does not prove a cause and effect relationship. Another big fallacy is the flimsy evidence provided by the author for his claim. By citing the fact that the advertisements of motorcycle X do not emphasize the noise of the motorcycle, the author assumes that buyers don't purchase motorcycle X for its exceptionally loud noise. Advertisements are not necessarily representative of buyer behavior; rather, they project the kind of behavior that companies want to encourage in the buyers.

Had the author wanted to make a better case, he should have provided better evidence, evidence establishing without doubt that the foreign company did intentionally copy motorcycle X to attract motorcycle X customers. He could have conducted polls on buyers of both motorcycle X and its copy. Further, the author's case could have been buttressed by comparisons of sales of another motorcycle and its copy, rather than a car and its copy. The author seems to have ignored buyer behavior by not considering factors such as brand loyalty, preferences, celebrity endorsements, and general performance of the vehicles. Most of all, the author should have delved deeper into why exactly motorcycle X has been successful enough to have been around for 70 years and what its imitator specifically lacks, feature for feature, with comparisons of price and target markets as well.

In conclusion, had the author not been so focused on negating a specific opinion, a better argument could have been constructed by discussing the aspects mentioned above and providing proper substantiation for each of the points made. In its current state, the argument is riddled with flaws and based on tangential issues.

4.6   Essay 6 (Middle-aged consumer)

> *The following appeared in the opinion column of a financial magazine.*
>
> "On average, middle-aged consumers devote 39 percent of their retail expenditure to department store products and services, while for younger consumers the average is only 25 percent. Since the number of middle-aged people will increase dramatically within the next decade, department stores can expect retail sales to increase significantly during that period. Furthermore, to take advantage of the trend, these stores should begin to replace some of those products intended to attract the younger consumer with products intended to attract the middle-aged consumer."
>
> *Discuss how well reasoned you find this argument. In your discussion be sure to analyze the line of reasoning and the use of evidence in the argument. For example, you may need to consider what questionable assumptions underlie the thinking and what alternative explanations or counterexamples might weaken the conclusion. You can also discuss what sort of evidence would strengthen or refute the argument, what changes in the argument would make it more logically sound, and what, if anything, would help you better evaluate its conclusion.*

Understand the argument

The writer states that middle-aged consumers spend a higher percentage of their retail expenditure in department stores than do younger consumers. He also states that the number of middle-aged people will increase dramatically within the next decade. Therefore, the department stores will make more in retail sales. To benefit from the demographic trend, the stores should replace their products to attract the middle-aged consumer rather than the younger consumer.

Faulty assumptions

- 39% of the retail expenditure of middle-aged consumers is higher than 25% of the retail expenditure of younger consumers

- The number of younger consumers will not also increase in the next decade

- Department stores cannot choose to attract both middle-aged consumers and younger consumers

Missing evidence

- Actual average amount of the retail expenditure of both middle-aged consumers and younger consumers

- Actual data on the increase of the number of middle-aged people for the next decade, as well as the expected number of younger people for the next decade

- The sales figures of department stores to analyze whom they cater to most and whether they can cater to both middle-aged consumers and younger consumers

Counter-examples

· What if the retail expenditure of middle-aged consumers is a far smaller amount than that of younger consumers?

· What if the number of younger consumers is also going to significantly increase in the next decade?

· What if department stores can successfully cater to both middle-aged consumers and younger consumers?

The essay

A contributor to a financial magazine opines that department stores can expect significant increases from the middle-aged consumer sector, and suggests a way to take advantage of the trend. While the argument appears plausible, it is only superficially so, as it lacks hard numbers and follows a dubious line of reasoning, thereby leading to an invalid conclusion.

To begin with, the writer has provided only percentages on the spending habits of middle-aged consumers and younger consumers. The claim that middle-aged consumers spend a higher percent of their retail expenditure in department stores than do younger consumers is meaningless in the absence of the amount of money spent by each segment. The writer seems to imply than 39 % of any number will always be higher than 25% of any other number. Percentages can never provide a true picture in the absence of actual numbers.

Another flaw on the writer's part is his prediction that the number of middle-aged people will "...increase dramatically..." without either furnishing supporting data or providing corresponding figures for the younger segment to help evaluate the prediction. The writer does not explicitly deny that the number of younger consumers will increase, leaving open the possibility that the number of younger consumers could also dramatically rise.

Finally, the writer exhorts the department stores to replace some of those products meant to attract the younger consumer with products for the middle-aged consumer. Why can't the department store choose to attract both middle-aged consumers and younger consumers? The writer clearly thinks the stores should not, without specifying the reason.

To sum up, the writer's claims might have been valid had he not based his predictions on incomplete, and therefore flawed, data. If the writer took into account the statistical requirements as outlined above, the argument would be far sounder than it is now.

4.7 Essay 7 (Corporate newsletter)

The following appeared in the editorial section of a corporate newsletter.

"The common notion that workers are generally apathetic about management issues is false, or at least outdated: a recently published survey indicates that 79 percent of the nearly 1,200 workers who responded to survey questionnaires expressed a high level of interest in the topics of corporate restructuring and redesign of benefits program."

Discuss how well reasoned you find this argument. In your discussion be sure to analyze the line of reasoning and the use of evidence in the argument. For example, you may need to consider what questionable assumptions underlie the thinking and what alternative explanations or counterexamples might weaken the conclusion. You can also discuss what sort of evidence would strengthen or refute the argument, what changes in the argument would make it more logically sound, and what, if anything, would help you better evaluate its conclusion.

Understand the argument

An editor refutes the general belief that workers are unconcerned about management issues. The editor makes his claim on the basis of a survey in which 79 percent of the 1,200 workers showed a high level of interest in the topics of corporate restructuring and redesign of benefits programs—topics that used to be very specific to management and senior level employees The reference of 79% of 1200 workers is cited to make you feel that it is high figure, thus the claim made is substantiated.

Faulty assumptions

- These 1200 workers are representative of workers in general

- Expressing interest in corporate restructuring and redesign of benefits programs is equal to being concerned about management issues

- The survey is unbiased, and trustworthy

Missing evidence

- Proof that the 1200 workers are representative of workers in general, that they include workers from every industry, every hierarchy-level, every demographic, etc

- Proof of workers' interest in other management issues in which the workers are not involved at all

Counter-examples

- What if the workers are all from a single division in the same company, thereby not representing even one company entirely, let alone workers in general?

· What if the workers expressed interest in corporate restructuring and redesign of benefits programs only because they will be impacted by it?

· What if the workers are still apathetic about other management issues?

The essay

An editor has claimed to debunk a common notion using data from a survey. The notion in question is that workers are unconcerned about management issues. The claim suffers from severe flawed assumptions in its use of data.

A primary concern with the given data that 79 percent of the 1,200 workers expressed a high level of interest in the topics of corporate restructuring and redesign of benefits programs is the lack of discussion on whether and how these 1200 workers are adequately representative of workers in general. Without any information about the workers, about their companies, specific departments, designation, job description, and other aspects, evaluating whether the survey can be admitted as valid evidence is impossible. Either the editor should prove that the 1200 workers are indeed representative or the survey should increase its reach to include a sufficient number of workers of every subtype to become representative.

Of equal concern is the assumption that interest expressed in some specific issues by some workers is commensurate to being interested in the general issue. That some of the surveyed workers expressed interest in corporate restructuring and redesign of benefits programs is not sufficient proof that they are necessarily concerned about management issues. The topics used by the survey are of as much relevance to management as they are to workers, therefore classifying these topics as strictly management issues is unjustified. The survey should widen its scope to a spread of management issues and record detailed responses from workers.

A tertiary but admissible concern is the methods employed by the surveyors. Analyzing the specific questionnaires used in the survey is important in determining whether the questions are capable of ascertaining the interest and concern of workers. Ticking some questions with positive responses is hardly the same as answering highly specific questions in great detail. Thus, the actual questionnaires would clarify such ambiguities.

In conclusion, since the editorial has chosen to cite merely one survey of 1200 workers to dispel a general belief affecting possibly a billion workers, accepting the editorial's claims seems difficult. Had there been specifics of the nature discussed above, the claim would have been much stronger.

4.8 Essay 8 (Stomach acid)

> *The following appeared in an article in a consumer-products magazine.*
>
> "Two of today's best-selling brands of full-strength prescription medication for the relief of excess stomach acid, Acid-Ease and Pepticaid, are now available in milder nonprescription forms. Doctors have written 76 million more prescriptions for full-strength Acid-Ease than for full-strength Pepticaid. So people who need an effective but milder nonprescription medication for the relief of excess stomach acid should choose Acid-Ease."
>
> *Discuss how well reasoned you find this argument. In your discussion be sure to analyze the line of reasoning and the use of evidence in the argument. For example, you may need to consider what questionable assumptions underlie the thinking and what alternative explanations or counterexamples might weaken the conclusion. You can also discuss what sort of evidence would strengthen or refute the argument, what changes in the argument would make it more logically sound, and what, if anything, would help you better evaluate its conclusion.*

Understand the argument

Best-selling brands of full-strength medication for the relief of excess stomach acid, Acid-Ease and Pepticaid, can only be prescribed to patients by doctors. The brands have also been launched in their milder versions and patients do not need a prescription from doctors to obtain them.

A writer in a consumer-products magazine claims that nonprescription Acid-Ease is more effective than nonprescription Pepticaid, and consumers should choose Acid-Ease for the relief of excess stomach acid. He makes this claim based on evidence that doctors have written 76 million more prescriptions for full-strength Acid-Ease than for full-strength Pepticaid.

Faulty assumptions

- Acid-Ease is better than Pepticaid because doctors write more prescriptions for Acid-Ease

- Full-strength prescription medication is equal to milder nonprescription forms in its efficacy

- Best-selling brands are the most effective brands

Missing evidence

- Proof about qualitative differences between Acid-Ease and Pepticaid

- Proof that milder Acid-Ease would be just as effective as full-strength Acid-Ease

- Information about why doctors prescribe more Acid-Ease than Pepticaid

- Information about the other brands in the market

Counter-examples

· What if Acid-Ease and Pepticaid are the same in their composition?

· What if milder Acid-Ease is not as effective as full-strength Acid-Ease?

· What if doctors prescribe more Acid-Ease only because it is better known than Pepticaid?

· What if some third brand has the most effective medication?

The essay

A writer in a consumer-products magazine asks consumers to choose the milder non-prescription form of a particular brand over that of another based on some data furnished about full-strength versions of those brands. The argument is highly vulnerable to criticism because it is based on faulty assumptions and lack of substantiation.

To start with, merely stating that one should choose Acid-Ease is imprecise if one is to rely only on the fact that doctors have written 76 million more prescriptions for full-strength Acid-Ease than for full-strength Pepticaid, especially so given the lack of any other information about said medications. Specific differences between Acid-Ease and Pepticaid, differences in composition, efficacy, side effects, price, etc, need to be ascertained before one is deemed better than the other. Further, determining why doctors prescribe full-strength Acid-Ease more than they do full-strength Pepticaid will also clarify whether Acid-Ease is truly more effective or simply better known to doctors than is Pepticaid. Also, as additional support, the writer should have mentioned the other brands of medication for the relief of excess stomach acid, and compared them to Acid-Ease and Pepticaid. Simply comparing two best-selling brands implies that effectiveness is determined by how well a particular brand sells.

Another fallacy in the article is that the claims are made about nonprescription forms of medication but the supporting data is given for full-strength prescription medication, implying that both forms of medication are similar in their characteristics. This is a dangerous presupposition implying that because full-strength Acid-Ease is supposedly better than full-strength Peticaid, the milder form of Acid-Ease will necessarily be better than comparable Pepticaid too. Before making these claims, the writer should explain the qualitative and quantitative differences between the two forms of each strength of the medications.

In conclusion, the article should have furnished a lot more data and made far fewer assumptions than it has. If the writer had done a thorough analysis of the differences between Acid-Ease and Pepticaid in both their milder and full-strength forms, as well as compared them with the other brands on the market, the argument would have been far stronger. As a result of these flaws, the article is utterly unconvincing in its current state.

4.9   Essay 9 (Ethical behavior by companies)

The following is an excerpt from a memo written by the head of a governmental department.

"Neither stronger ethics regulations nor stronger enforcement mechanisms are necessary to ensure ethical behavior by companies doing business with this department. We already have a code of ethics that companies doing business with this department are urged to abide by, and virtually all of these companies have agreed to follow it. We also know that the code is relevant to the current business environment because it was approved within the last year, and in direct response to specific violations committed by companies with which we were then working—not in abstract anticipation of potential violations, as so many such codes are."

Discuss how well reasoned you find this argument. In your discussion be sure to analyze the line of reasoning and the use of evidence in the argument. For example, you may need to consider what questionable assumptions underlie the thinking and what alternative explanations or counterexamples might weaken the conclusion. You can also discuss what sort of evidence would strengthen or refute the argument, what changes in the argument would make it more logically sound, and what, if anything, would help you better evaluate its conclusion.

Understand the argument

A memo from the head of a governmental department claims that they do not need stronger ethics regulations or stronger enforcement mechanisms to ensure ethical behavior by companies doing business with this department. This is because the department already has a code of ethics that companies doing business have agreed to follow. He emphasizes that the code of ethics is relevant because it was approved last year, after deliberating on specific violations committed by companies with which the department was then working. The code addresses the violations committed by the companies then. He opines that the code is better because it is specifically designed and does not deal with abstract potential violations.

Faulty assumptions

· Agreeing to follow a code necessarily implies that everyone will follow it

· The companies will not commit violations other than those mentioned in the code

· Stronger ethics regulations or stronger enforcement mechanisms have no other positive effects when used, effects such as deterring possible offenders

· The department would not work with any other company in the future other than the ones who have agreed to follow the code

Missing evidence

· Proof such as agreements that companies will follow the specific code

- Information about all possible violations than can be committed and about which ones the specific code deals with

- Details about the possibilities of working with other companies

Counter-examples

- What if the companies do not follow the specific code?

- What if they follow the specific code but violate some other regulation?

- What if the government department has to deal with other companies in the future who may or may not agree to the specific code?

The essay

A memo from the head of a governmental department claims that it does not need strong ethics regulations or enforcement mechanisms because it has designed a code that deals with the violations committed by the companies it worked with last year. The companies it is working with now have agreed to abide by that specific code. The argument is riddled with flawed assumptions, leaving it completely invalid.

To begin with, dispensing with regulations or enforcement mechanisms in favor of a code implies that these things are mutually exclusive. Typically, codes only serve a directional purpose, informing the concerned parties of the expected behavior. Strong regulations and enforcement mechanisms are needed to have an enforceable deterrent effect and reinforce the desired behavior. It is clearly in any entity's best interests to have all these devices to achieve the maximum effect.

Another flawed assumption in the memo is the simplistic view taken by the department head. Assuming that companies would necessarily follow the code just because they say so is rather silly. If the department head had extracted some contracts or agreements from those companies about following the code, the idea wouldn't sound so absurd.

Further, the highly specific nature of said code presents an equally problematic issue with the whole proposition. The code is specifically designed to address the violations committed by the companies that were working with the governmental department last year, assuming that all companies that will ever work with the governmental department will commit the same violations. The memo conspicuously does not discuss at all the possibility that the current companies can commit violations other than the ones addressed in the specific code.

Finally, even if all that the memo says is to be believed, what would happen if the governmental department works with other companies at a later date? Whether they will agree to the specific code is a risk that will have to be taken in the absence of a more general, abstract code dealing with all potential violations, or of regulations or enforcement mechanisms.

In conclusion, the department head has taken a completely myopic view of the situation and has ignored common sense altogether. Abstract laws and regulations are so designed to ensure that all, or at least most, violations fall within the scope of those laws. Designing specific codes as an additional safeguard is not bad, but to use the code instead of general safeguards is inviting deep trouble. Consequently, if this memo is heeded, a state of jungle law may soon descend.

4.10 Essay 10 (Saluda Natural Spring Water)

The following appeared in an article in a health and fitness magazine.

"Laboratory studies show that Saluda Natural Spring Water contains several of the minerals necessary for good health and that it is completely free of bacteria. Residents of Saluda, the small town where the water is bottled, are hospitalized less frequently than the national average. Even though Saluda Natural Spring Water may seem expensive, drinking it instead of tap water is a wise investment in good health."

Discuss how well reasoned you find this argument. In your discussion be sure to analyze the line of reasoning and the use of evidence in the argument. For example, you may need to consider what questionable assumptions underlie the thinking and what alternative explanations or counterexamples might weaken the conclusion. You can also discuss what sort of evidence would strengthen or refute the argument, what changes in the argument would make it more logically sound, and what, if anything, would help you better evaluate its conclusion.

Understand the argument

In an article in a health and fitness magazine, a writer claims that replacing tap water with expensive Saluda Spring Water is a worthwhile investment. To support this claim, he provides information about the residents of the town of Saluda, where Saluda Spring Water is bottled. These residents have a lower frequency of hospitalizations than the national average. The author also states that Saluda Spring Water contains many necessary minerals and is completely free of bacteria. The author acknowledges the fact that Saluda Spring Water is expensive but maintains that it is worth investing in for good health.

Faulty assumptions

· The water of Saluda is the primary reason for the people of the town Saluda not getting hospitalized as often; no other factor is significant in the less frequent hospitalizations of residents of Saluda

· Less frequent hospitalizations mean good health

· Spending money on Saluda Spring Water is cheaper than getting hospitalized often

Missing evidence

· Details about other factors that may affect the frequency of hospitalizations

· Proof about how specifically the water reduces the frequency of hospitalizations and leads to good health

· Details about whether Saluda Spring Water has been purified to remove all impurities other than bacteria

Counter-examples

- What if some other dietary, environmental, or genetic factor is responsible for the lower frequency of hospitalization in residents of Saluda?

- What if residents of Saluda fall ill just as often as any other town's residents but are not hospitalized as frequently?

- What if it is cheaper to get hospitalized a few extra times than it is to drink only Saluda Spring Water instead of tap water?

- What if Saluda Spring Water contains microorganisms other than bacteria?

The essay

In a magazine article, a writer claims that replacing tap water with expensive Saluda Spring Water is a good and worthwhile investment. The writer provides some facts about Saluda Spring Water and about the residents of the town of Saluda, where the water is bottled, to support this claim. The argument is completely unconvincing because it relies on incomplete evidence and flawed assumptions.

To begin with, the writer uses as primary support the fact that the frequency of hospitalizations for residents of Saluda, the town where the water is bottled, is lower than the national average. He is relying on the faulty assumption that because residents get hospitalized less frequently, the water must be the cause of that. Two coincidental observations cannot be necessarily termed cause and effect unless causality is proven. The writer should have analyzed all possible factors for lower frequency of hospitalizations before claiming that the water is responsible for the same. In the same vein, that fact used by the author to support his claim implies that lower frequency of hospitalizations is equivalent to good health. In a small town, as Saluda may well be, a more likely cause of lower frequency of hospitalizations is probably fewer hospitals or doctors rather than better health! Fewer hospitalizations do not mean that residents are in better health. It is also possible that residents get sick as often as those from any other place, but just don't get hospitalized or are not treated as seriously. Conversely, it can also imply that elsewhere people might get hospitalized for trivial things. Unless these details are sifted through, one cannot assume that a lower number of hospitalizations is an indicator of health.

Another problem with the argument is the reliance on partial evidence. The writer states that Saluda water contains many important minerals and is free of bacteria. However, what about the other microbial possibilities that can also make a person quite sick? Does Saluda Spring Water have traces of viruses, algae, or fungi? These niggling doubts make the whole claim dubious. Additionally, the author mentions that Saluda Spring Water is costly but worth the investment in good health. This claim needs some hard data for support because water is not a once-in-a-blue-moon requirement; it is an item of daily consumption, and in considerable quantities. So, if Saluda Spring Water is expensive, would it be cheaper to pay hospital bills every so often than to drink costly Saluda Spring Water on a daily basis? Not dealing with this possibility leaves the argument vulnerable.

To conclude, the author has taken a lot of information for granted and failed to deal with numerous aspects in making his claim. Had he taken into consideration the above factors and accordingly supported his claim with proper evidence and without assumptions, the argument would have been sound and convincing.

4.11 Essay 11 (Waymarsh students)

> *The following appeared in the editorial section of a local newspaper.*
>
> "This past winter, 200 students from Waymarsh State College traveled to the state capitol building to protest against proposed cuts in funding for various state college programs. The other 12,000 Waymarsh students evidently weren't so concerned about their education: they either stayed on campus or left for winter break. Since the group who did not protest is far more numerous, it is more representative of the state's college students than are the protesters. Therefore the state legislature need not heed the appeals of the protesting students."
>
> *Discuss how well reasoned you find this argument. In your discussion be sure to analyze the line of reasoning and the use of evidence in the argument. For example, you may need to consider what questionable assumptions underlie the thinking and what alternative explanations or counterexamples might weaken the conclusion. You can also discuss what sort of evidence would strengthen or refute the argument, what changes in the argument would make it more logically sound, and what, if anything, would help you better evaluate its conclusion.*

Understand the argument

In the editorial, the writer claims that since only 200 students from Waymarsh State College turned up to protest against the cuts in funding for state colleges, while the other 12000 were either at the college or away for winter break, the students are not really concerned about the issue. The author also suggests that the 12000 who weren't protesting are not concerned about their education. The primary claim is that the legislature should not have to concede to the protesters.

Faulty assumptions

- 200 students are not representative of the students from Waymarsh State College

- Only those 200 students who showed up at the protest are concerned about their education

- Number of students is the deciding factor in what represents the students' wishes

- State legislature should make decisions based only on majority's wishes

Missing evidence

- Information about whether the 200 students are not representative of all the students of the college

- Views of the students regarding the proposed cuts in funding for state colleges

- Details about the impact of the proposed cuts and various factors involved in the decision

Counter-examples

- What if those 200 students were nominated by all the students to protest against the cuts in funding for state colleges?

- What if the other students also don't want cuts in funding for state colleges to be implemented?

- What if some other factors prove the proposed cuts in funding for state colleges a bad decision?

The essay

In an editorial, the author exhorts the state legislature not to accede to the demands of the protesters, by providing data evidently in support of his opinion. While the claim may sound valid on initial evaluation, a more detailed analysis reveals that it is based on partial evidence and flawed assumptions, leaving the argument fallacious.

To begin with, the primary evidence used by the author in support of his claim that the majority of students don't wish to protest against the cuts in funding for state colleges is the fact that only 200 Waymarsh students turned up at the protest. He goes on point out that 12000 other students from the same college were either at school or away on winter break, implying that the bigger number represents the views of the majority. However, the author seems to have completely missed the possibility that the 200 that did turn up may have done so as representatives of all the students at the college. For the students to protest against something, not all have to turn up to actually protest. Some could have been nominated to do so, while others may have been running other campaigns online, or in person. Unless this possibility is fully explored and proof obtained that the other 12000 had no interest whatsoever in protesting against the cuts in funding for state colleges, one cannot assume that they wish the cuts to be implemented. The author should conduct a survey of the students who did not show up and fully ascertain their wishes instead of taking the same for granted.

Another minor point that deserves mentioning is the fact that the author urges the state legislature to act upon what he thinks are the wishes of the majority of the students. All factors being equal, it is a good idea to take into account the wishes of the majority. Nevertheless, the author does not provide any information about the implications and repercussions of the proposed cuts in funding for state colleges. To urge the legislature to make a decision based solely on the majority's wishes, without considering all possible aspects, does not make for a very good plan of action. The author should explicitly discuss all the possibilities of the proposed cuts and prove that no factor other than the majority's wishes remains to be evaluated before urging the state legislature to make its decision. Even at that, majority or minority, all valid opinions must be taken into account before passing any legislation.

To conclude, the author may have been making a valid claim, but it is completely overshadowed by the fact that he relies on hasty assumptions. The lack of substantiation for his views leaves the entire claim vulnerable. Had the author taken into account the aspects discussed above, the argument would have been much stronger than it is now.

4.12 Essay 12 (Taxes on railways)

> *The following appeared as part of an editorial in an industry newsletter.*
>
> "While trucking companies that deliver goods pay only a portion of highway maintenance costs and no property tax on the highways they use, railways spend billions per year maintaining and upgrading their facilities. The government should lower the railroad companies' property taxes, since sending goods by rail is clearly a more appropriate mode of ground transportation than highway shipping. For one thing, trains consume only a third of the fuel a truck would use to carry the same load, making them a more cost-effective and environmentally sound mode of transport. Furthermore, since rail lines already exist, increases in rail traffic would not require building new lines at the expense of taxpaying citizens."
>
> *Discuss how well reasoned you find this argument. In your discussion be sure to analyze the line of reasoning and the use of evidence in the argument. For example, you may need to consider what questionable assumptions underlie the thinking and what alternative explanations or counterexamples might weaken the conclusion. You can also discuss what sort of evidence would strengthen or refute the argument, what changes in the argument would make it more logically sound, and what, if anything, would help you better evaluate its conclusion.*

Understand the argument

In an editorial in an industry newsletter, a writer claims that the government should lower the property taxes levied on railroad companies. The primary reason for this claim is that trucking companies use highways and pay only a part of highway maintenance costs but no property tax on the highways, while railways incur a cost of billions to maintain and upgrade their facilities. Another supporting premise given by the writer is that trains use only one-third of the fuel that a truck would use to carry the load carried by the train. So, the writer tries to prove that railways are more cost-effective and better for the environment than trucks. The final piece of support is that even if more people start using railways to transport their goods, no new rail lines will need to be built because they already exist.

Faulty assumptions

- Railway services are comparable to trucking services. The goods transported by trucking companies can easily be dealt with by railways

- The goods transported by the trucking companies need to be delivered only to places that are within the reach of railways

- No other entity uses highways as considerably as trucking companies

Missing evidence

- Details about the quantity of goods transported by trucking companies

· Specifics about the destinations serviced by trucking companies and whether railways are available to transport to those points

· Details about the use of highways and what proportion of that use is by the trucking companies

Counter-examples

· What if the trucking companies' use of highways makes up a very small portion compared to other entities' uses, but the companies pay a bigger chunk of taxes?

· What if the railways don't transport to the destinations serviced by the trucking companies?

· What if the people who employ trucking companies to transport goods have only small quantities to be transported at any one time, but to multiple destinations?

· What if it is cheaper for people to transport goods via trucks than it is via railways?

The essay

A writer for an editorial in an industry newsletter suggests that the government reduce the property taxes levied on railways. The writer provides numerous pieces of evidence in support of this claim. While the suggestion may seem to carry weight, the flawed assumptions and lack of substantiation have left the argument difficult to heed.

To begin with, the chief support employed by the writer to claim that the government should reduce the property taxes levied on railways is to point out that trucking companies seem to have it easy. The writer states that trucking companies don't have to pay property taxes and have to pay only a portion of highway maintenance costs, and so railways that spend billions upgrading and maintaining their own facilities should be exempted from property taxes. Before making this claim, the author should have established the comparability of trucking and railroad companies in this particular aspect. In fact, the trucking and railroad companies have to pay different amounts of tax precisely because the nature of their use is different. Trucking companies should have to pay only a portion of highway maintenance costs because they do not have exclusive access to highways; however, railroad companies lay their rail lines and use the lines themselves or lease them to another company, but either way, use is private and exclusive. Further, the trucking companies should not have to pay property taxes because they do not build any immovable structures on the highways they use; in contrast, the railways should have to pay property taxes because these companies lay rail lines on land and property, rendering the property unusable for almost any other thing. Considering these aspects, it is preposterous to suggest that the government should reduce the property taxes levied on the railways because the trucking companies don't have to pay property taxes and have to pay only a portion of highway maintenance taxes.

Another flawed assumption on the part of the writer is the suggestion that railways can completely replace trucking companies in moving goods, and can do so in a cheaper way for comparable amounts of load. While this may be true theoretically, in practice it is difficult to implement. There are many points of difference to consider before evaluating this claim. The first point is the destinations serviced by the trucking companies. The trucks will deliver goods from point A to point B, but trains will only deliver goods from a railroad station near point A to a railroad station near point B. From the station to the actual destination, the transporters will need to hire trucks. The second point to consider is the quantity of goods usually transported by people who employ trucking companies. Such people usually have smaller loads that need to be delivered to different destinations all over the States. Using trains for smaller loads meant for different destinations is an inefficient use of resources. The upshot is that trains are the best means of transport for those who are looking to transport bigger loads to a fixed destination, and trucks are the best way for anyone looking to move smaller amounts of goods to different destinations. To merely compare the amount of fuel consumed by trucks and trains for a certain amount of goods is not the correct way to determine the cheaper mode.

To conclude, the writer should have provided a case for railways without trying to force a comparison between the trucking and the railroad companies. If he wished to compare the two, he should have taken into consideration the factors discussed above. Had he done so, his argument would have been far stronger than it is now.

4.13 Essay 13 (Illegal use of cocaine)

> *The following appeared in the editorial section of a newspaper.*
>
> "As public concern over drug abuse has increased, authorities have become more vigilant in their efforts to prevent illegal drugs from entering the country. Many drug traffickers have consequently switched from marijuana, which is bulky, or heroin, which has a market too small to justify the risk of severe punishment, to cocaine. Thus enforcement efforts have ironically resulted in an observed increase in the illegal use of cocaine."
>
> *Discuss how well reasoned you find this argument. In your discussion be sure to analyze the line of reasoning and the use of evidence in the argument. For example, you may need to consider what questionable assumptions underlie the thinking and what alternative explanations or counterexamples might weaken the conclusion. You can also discuss what sort of evidence would strengthen or refute the argument, what changes in the argument would make it more logically sound, and what, if anything, would help you better evaluate its conclusion.*

Understand the argument

An editorial claims that enforcement efforts of authorities are directly responsible for increased use of cocaine. To support this claim, the editor provides the context that because of increased concern over drug use, authorities have stepped up their efforts to stop drugs from entering the country. According to the editor, because of these increased efforts, drug traffickers have switched from marijuana or heroin to cocaine. The editor states that marijuana is bulky, and the risk of punishment is not worth the small market commanded by heroin, and so the drug traffickers have switched to cocaine.

Faulty assumptions

- The authorities are being vigilant enough when it comes to marijuana and heroin but not when it comes to cocaine

- The increased use of cocaine is a direct result of the vigilant efforts of authorities

- Cocaine is not bulky and has a large enough market to justify the risk of punishment

- Cocaine use has increased only because of enforcement efforts

Missing evidence

- The extent to which enforcement efforts include trying to prevent cocaine

- Details about why enforcement efforts are not successful in preventing the trafficking of cocaine

- Other aspects that may have led to an increase in the use of cocaine

Counter-examples

· What if some other factors led to the increased use of cocaine?

· What if only the recent scrutiny has revealed the extent of cocaine use, which was at the same level all along?

The essay

An editorial claims that vigilant efforts of authorities have directly led to increased use of cocaine. This claim is supported by a couple of premises. Nevertheless, the given premises do not justify the claim being made by the editor because the claim relies heavily on multiple assumptions and suffers from a severe lack of evidence.

To begin with, the editor links the increased use of cocaine to increased enforcement efforts to prevent drugs from entering the country without stating explicitly how. Merely stating that two events have happened does not make one the cause and the other the result. Cause-and-effect relationships cannot be assumed, but need to be proven. There could be other reasons that cocaine consumption has gone up – reasons such as the fact that cocaine is easier to manufacture, or that it is cheaper than other drugs. Merely linking increased cocaine use with increased enforcement efforts is unconvincing.

Another problem is the multiple assumptions in the editor's claim. The first assumption that comes to light is that while enforcement efforts seem to have checked the use of marijuana and heroin, they have been unsuccessful in preventing the entry of cocaine to the country. Details about these operations are needed to understand this conundrum. Another assumption comes to light when the editor explains that cocaine is favored by drug traffickers because marijuana is bulky, and heroin is not in enough demand for traffickers to risk severe punishment, implying but not stating that cocaine is not necessarily bulky, and either has a big enough market to risk severe punishment, or that punishment for trafficking cocaine is not as severe. These are serious assumptions that need to be explicitly dealt with, and not left as natural assumptions.

Further, the editorial claims that the enforcement efforts have had the ironic result of an observed increase in the use of cocaine, implying that there's no proof that the use of cocaine did indeed increase recently. The use of the word "observed" leads one to wonder whether the increased use of cocaine has just been observed recently or has it actually increased recently? It is possible that the currently observed levels of cocaine use were present all along, but the current level of public attention merely brought those levels to light. The argument should have provided concrete proof that the use of cocaine has actually gone up, instead of merely claiming so.

To conclude, the editor could have been making a valid point, but the validity is muddied by the use of numerous assumptions and a paucity of requisite information to justify the claims. If the author had considered the points discussed above, the claim would have been justified.

4.14 Essay 14 (Waymarsh University)

The following appeared as part of an article in the education section of a Waymarsh city newspaper.

"Throughout the last two decades, those who earned graduate degrees found it very difficult to get jobs teaching their academic specialties at the college level. Those with graduate degrees from Waymarsh University had an especially hard time finding such jobs. But better times are coming in the next decade for all academic job seekers, including those from Waymarsh. Demographic trends indicate that an increasing number of people will be reaching college age over the next 10 years; consequently, we can expect that the job market will improve dramatically for people seeking college-level teaching positions in their fields."

Discuss how well reasoned you find this argument. In your discussion be sure to analyze the line of reasoning and the use of evidence in the argument. For example, you may need to consider what questionable assumptions underlie the thinking and what alternative explanations or counterexamples might weaken the conclusion. You can also discuss what sort of evidence would strengthen or refute the argument, what changes in the argument would make it more logically sound, and what, if anything, would help you better evaluate its conclusion.

Understand the argument

An article writer for the education section of a Waymarsh city newspaper claims that academic job seekers will find teaching jobs in their fields in the next decade, even those graduates who are from Waymarsh University. This claim is based on data that shows that the number of people reaching college age will increase in the next decade. So, even though academic job seekers, especially those from Waymarsh University, have found it difficult up til now to find teaching jobs in their academic specialties at the college level, things will soon change.

Faulty assumptions

- The number of people applying for teaching jobs in the next decade will not increase significantly

- A significant number of people reaching college age will opt for college education

- The number of people reaching college age will choose to study in the specific fields in which the job seekers had found difficult to get jobs

- Academic job seekers from Waymarsh University will not find it harder than usual to find teaching jobs in their fields in the next decade

Missing evidence

- Demographic trends for academic job seekers in the next decade

- Details of possible preferences of the people reaching college age in the next decade

· Specifics about why academic job seekers from Waymarsh University find it harder than usual to find teaching jobs in their fields

Counter-examples

· What if the number of academic job seekers is also going to increase significantly in the next decade?

· What if many of the people reaching college age decide not to opt for college education?

· What if many of the people reaching college age decide not to opt for the specific fields in which the job seekers have found difficult to get jobs?

· What if graduate academic job seekers from Waymarsh University don't get teaching jobs in their fields even after the number of people enrolled in colleges goes up?

The essay

In the education section of a Waymarsh city newspaper, a writer claims that better times are ahead for academic job seekers, implying that teaching jobs in desired academic specialties at the college level will become available. This prediction is based on data from demographic trends. While the argument may seem convincing, a more detailed analysis reveals that it is based on partial evidence, and relies on assumptions, leaving the prediction unsure.

To begin with, the writer bases his claims solely on the fact that the number of people reaching college age will increase in the next decade. Relying only on this piece of data for the prediction that teaching jobs in desired academic specialties at the college level will increase brings up two unsubstantiated assumptions. One assumption is that since the number of people reaching college age will increase, the number of people who actually opt for college education will also increase commensurately. It does not have to be so. The second assumption is that while the number of people reaching college age will increase in the next decade, the number of academic job seekers will not also increase significantly in that time period. If the number of academic job seekers also increases, the level of competition remains intact, leaving it just as hard for those who are looking for teaching jobs in specific academic specialties at the college level to find them, as it is now. Without proof that negates these two possibilities, and just assuming that these possibilities will not occur, the argument is left open to criticism.

Another problem in the argument is that the writer merely tries to present a resolution to a problem in a highly cosmetic way. The problem is that graduate academic job seekers, especially those who are from Waymarsh University, cannot find teaching positions in their desired academic specialties at the college level. Without any investigation of why this is so, the writer presents a predicted demographic trend and suggests that the problem will go away on its own. To actually be helpful, the writer should have analyzed the reason for the job seekers not getting teaching jobs in their specific fields and then presented an analysis of all possible remedies. Simply throwing incomplete demographic statistics will not make the problem go away.

To conclude, the writer's attempt to replace actual analysis with possible demographic data left his prediction riddled with fallacies. As a result, the argument is wholly unconvincing. Had the author taken into account the points discussed above, the argument would have seemed logical and sound.

4.15   Essay 15 (Einstein High School)

The following appeared in a speech delivered by a member of the city council.

"Twenty years ago, only half of the students who graduated from Einstein High School went on to attend a college or university. Today, two-thirds of the students who graduate from Einstein do so. Clearly, Einstein has improved its educational effectiveness over the past two decades. This improvement has occurred despite the fact that the school's funding, when adjusted for inflation, is about the same as it was 20 years ago. Therefore, we do not need to make any substantial increase in the school's funding at this time."

Discuss how well reasoned you find this argument. In your discussion be sure to analyze the line of reasoning and the use of evidence in the argument. For example, you may need to consider what questionable assumptions underlie the thinking and what alternative explanations or counterexamples might weaken the conclusion. You can also discuss what sort of evidence would strengthen or refute the argument, what changes in the argument would make it more logically sound, and what, if anything, would help you better evaluate its conclusion.

Understand the argument

Details about the number of students who graduate from Einstein High School and go on to attend college have been given, both for the present time and for twenty years ago. Twenty years ago, only 50% of graduates went on to attend college, but now 66% do so. However, the funding in real money terms has remained unchanged. On the basis of these specifics, a member of the city council claims that since Einstein has improved its educational effectiveness despite no substantial change in funding, the city does not need to make any increase in the school's funding at this time.

Faulty assumptions

- The number of current students who graduate from Einstein and attend college has significantly increased from the number twenty years ago

- The number of students who graduate from Einstein High School and go on to attend a college or university is indicative of educational effectiveness

- No other factor is responsible for the increased number of students who have graduated from Einstein High School and gone on to attend a college or university

Missing evidence

- The total number of students who graduated from Einstein High School and went on to attend a college or university

- Details about factors that affect educational effectiveness, such as curriculum, exam patterns, etc.

· Specifics about other possible factors that could have been responsible for the increased number of students who graduated from Einstein High School and went on to attend a college or university

Counter-examples

· What if the total number of students who graduated from Einstein High School and went on to attend a college or university has declined?

· What if some other factor is responsible for the increased number of students who graduated from Einstein High School and went on to attend a college or university?

· What if increased funding can significantly improve factors that affect educational effectiveness, such as curriculum, teaching, and exam patterns?

The essay

In a speech, a city councilor claims that the city does not have to increase funding to Einstein High School, not in any considerable measure. The councillor makes these claims on the basis of some specifics that he provides. While the argument may seem convincing on initial evaluation, a more detailed analysis reveals that the specifics provided by the councilor are partial and thereby lead to a shaky conclusion.

To begin with, the councilor states that since the proportion of students who graduated from high school and went on to attend a college or university has increased despite no noticeable change in funding, Einstein must have improved its educational effectiveness, regardless of extra money. The councilor fails to connect the dots between graduates who attend college and educational effectiveness. The number of high school graduates who choose to eventually attend college can be affected by many factors other than educational effectiveness at their high schools. For instance, many people opt for improving educational qualifications whenever the economy is on a downturn, and a highly competitive job market can also get people seeking higher education. Any of these factors could have been equally responsible for the statistics provided by the councilor. Without specifically negating the play of these factors and linking the educational effectiveness of Einstein High School, the councilor's claims are unwarranted. Moreover, educational effectiveness is a concept that is entirely removed from the possibility of whether a student will seek further education. Educational effectiveness deals with the way the curriculum has been designed and the manner in which it is imparted, thereby affecting the student's absorption of the education. This effectiveness can be affected by a range of factors, beginning with funding and spanning to curriculum, examination patterns, and pedagogy, and ending with factors affecting students themselves. To link educational effectiveness with the proportion of high school graduates seeking college education seems illogical, especially in the face of no evidence connecting the two. A minor point also to be noted in the data given by the councilor is that proportions and percentages rarely present a complete picture by themselves. To elaborate, the proportion of students who graduated from Einstein High School and went on to attend a college or university may have increased, but the actual number of students who graduated from Einstein High School and went on to attend a college or university could have declined. Thus, the councillor should have backed his claims up with complete data, in numbers and percentages, on the number of students who graduated and went on to attend college.

To conclude, the councillor's argument suffers from the use of partial evidence and from faulty connections and assumptions. On the basis of given evidence, it is not possible to conclude whether or not the funding to Einstein High School should be increased. Had the councillor taken into account the factors discussed above, his claims would have been far stronger than they are now.

4.16 Essay 16 (Mammon Savings and Loan)

> *The following appeared in a memo from the customer service division to the manager of Mammon Savings and Loan.*
>
> "We believe that improved customer service is the best way for us to differentiate ourselves from competitors and attract new customers. We can offer our customers better service by reducing waiting time in teller lines from an average of six minutes to an average of three. By opening for business at 8:30 instead of 9:00, and by remaining open for an additional hour beyond our current closing time, we will be better able to accommodate the busy schedules of our customers. These changes will enhance our bank's image as the most customer friendly bank in town and give us the edge over our competition."
>
> *Discuss how well reasoned you find this argument. In your discussion be sure to analyze the line of reasoning and the use of evidence in the argument. For example, you may need to consider what questionable assumptions underlie the thinking and what alternative explanations or counterexamples might weaken the conclusion. You can also discuss what sort of evidence would strengthen or refute the argument, what changes in the argument would make it more logically sound, and what, if anything, would help you better evaluate its conclusion.*

Understand the argument

The customer service division of Mammon Savings and Loan believes that if the bank opens half an earlier and closes an hour later, then the waiting time in teller lines can be reduced from an average of six minutes to an average of three. If this change is brought about, the customer service division feels that customer service will be improved considerably, thereby attracting new customers and giving Mammon an edge over competitors. This move is also expected to improve the bank's image as the most customer friendly bank in town.

Faulty assumptions

- Increasing business hours will reduce the waiting time in teller lines from an average of six minutes to an average of three

- Competitors will not respond with similar measures to retain their image

- Customers will be able to benefit from the earlier opening time and later closing time

Missing evidence

- Details about what causes current waiting time in teller lines of an average of six minutes and how increasing the bank's hours will reduce waiting time in teller lines to an average of three

- Specifics about the competitor banks, their unique selling points, and whether they will respond to this move by implementing the same

- Proof that a sizable number of customers will come at 8:30 instead of 9:00 or in the extra hour after the current closing time

Counter-examples

- What if a sizable number of customers cannot come earlier than 9:00 or later in the extra hour after the current closing time?

- What if competitors also respond with a similar move and take the edge away from the bank?

- What if some factor other than number of working hours is responsible for the average of six minutes waiting time in teller lines? [inadequate technology support/fewer tellers]

The essay

The customer service department of Mammon Savings and Loan recommends that the bank increase its workings hours to attract new customers, distinguish Mammon from its competitors, and reduce average waiting time in teller lines. While the idea seems appealing upon first glance, deeper evaluation reveals multiple assumptions and lack of evidence, leaving the recommendation unsubstantiated.

To begin with, the primary reason that the customer service department furnishes in recommending increased working hours is to attract new customers and distinguish Mammon from its competitors in the customer service aspect. If that is the end goal of the entire move, then it is worth ascertaining whether Mammon's competitors are likely to respond with a similar move, taking away any advantage that Mammon can potentially gain. The answer to that should determine the effectiveness of the move. Further, to distinguish Mammon from its competitors in the customer service aspect, the department should survey customers and figure out specifics of what is desired by the customers, what competitors are providing that Mammon is not, and what other aspects Mammon can implement, instead of just randomly deciding to increase its working hours. Even if we assume that the move is feasible and do not discuss the logistical rearrangements the entire operation would involve, opening at 8:30 instead of 9:00 and closing an hour later would not necessarily reduce waiting time in teller lines from six minutes to three, not unless customers are willing to come in during those additional hours. If customers would prefer to wait, on average, 6 minutes instead of 3 minutes to avoid coming earlier or later, the plan would fail to achieve its objective. Instead, an analysis of the reasons behind the waiting time in teller lines should be done. Numerous reasons could be causing higher than average waiting time. For instance, if the tellers are not equipped with the latest technology to speed up the transactions, every transaction will contribute to a small delay, compounding in a noticeable way. Also, Mammon could think about setting up automated teller machines that can handle routine transactions such as deposits and withdrawals, updating account books, displaying transactions, etc., if the bank's offices do not already provide that. Such measures could achieve a reduction in waiting times in teller lines and improve the efficiency of the bank's operations, without needing the redistribution of resources that the recommended move would involve.

To conclude, the customer service department's recommendation cannot be evaluated thoroughly given the lack of requisite data and inadequate research on the need for the change. If the department takes into account the various aspects and considerations discussed above, the recommendation made by the department could be stronger and more logical.

4.17 Essay 17 (Quality of life)

The following appeared as part of an article in a magazine on lifestyles.

"Two years ago, City L was listed fourteenth in an annual survey that ranks cities according to the quality of life that can be enjoyed by those living in them. This information will enable people who are moving to the state in which City L is located to confidently identify one place, at least, where schools are good, housing is affordable, people are friendly, the environment is safe, and the arts flourish."

Discuss how well reasoned you find this argument. In your discussion be sure to analyze the line of reasoning and the use of evidence in the argument. For example, you may need to consider what questionable assumptions underlie the thinking and what alternative explanations or counterexamples might weaken the conclusion. You can also discuss what sort of evidence would strengthen or refute the argument, what changes in the argument would make it more logically sound, and what, if anything, would help you better evaluate its conclusion.

Understand the argument

An article writer claims that for anyone who is moving to the state in which City L is, City L is at least one good location that the person can rely on to have good schools, affordable housing, etc. The writer bases his claims on the fact that a two-year old survey ranked City L as the fourteenth place in rankings for quality of life.

Faulty assumptions

· City L still has the same attributes it had two years ago

· The survey is thoroughly representative and includes all parameters important in evaluating cities all over the country

Missing evidence

· Data about City L's current ranking and its qualities

· Specifics about the survey to evaluate whether it is representative

Counter-examples

· What if City L's current rank has slipped considerably?

· What if the survey was conducted using limited parameters and missed out on important ones?

The essay

An article writer claims that in the state in which City L is located, one guaranteed good place to move to is City L. This claim is premised upon a two-year old survey of places with a good quality of life in which City L stood fourteenth. A potentially good recommendation is marred by a woeful lack of evidence, leaving the argument dependent upon faulty assumptions.

To begin with, the claim that City L is a sure bet as a good place to move to, if one is contemplating a move to the state in which City L is located, is based entirely upon an annual survey that is already two years past. This survey is most likely outdated. The lack of information about the current rankings of City L is conspicuous. Furthermore, even if the rank of City L is unchanged from fourteenth, the survey itself remains of dubious quality until its credentials can be established. The article writer has not provided important information about the survey to enable the reader to judge its quality. The sample size, the surveyed parameters, and the evaluation period are some of the many factors that one needs to consider before the survey can be deemed trustworthy enough. Since none of these factors are explicitly clarified in the argument, the worth of the survey is unclear. Furthermore, the author mentions that City L has good schools, affordable housing, a safe environment, and a flourishing arts scene without specifying whether this information is just an assumption of his because of City L's rank in the two-year old survey or because he has actually ascertained that about City L by himself. All these ambiguities leave the whole proposition difficult to judge or accept.

To conclude, what the writer should have done is relied on better data, data that includes the maximum number of possible parameters factored into quality of life. For instance, factors such as crime rate, community development, the number and quality of educational institutions, the economy and availability of jobs, health and sanitation facilities, recreational options, etc. must be taken into account before determining the quality of life in a given location. Another important factor is that the writer should have used recent data, not a two-year old survey. Had the writer taken into account these aspects, his recommendation would have been much better than it is.

4.18 Essay 18 (Synthetic farm products)

> *The following was excerpted from the speech of a spokesperson for Synthetic Farm Products, Inc..*
>
> "Many farmers who invested in the equipment needed to make the switch from synthetic to organic fertilizers and pesticides feel that it would be too expensive to resume synthetic farming at this point. But studies of farmers who switched to organic farming last year indicate that their current crop yields are lower. Hence their purchase of organic farming equipment, a relatively minor investment compared to the losses that would result from continued lower crop yields, cannot justify persisting on an unwise course. And the choice to farm organically is financially unwise, given that it was motivated by environmental rather than economic concerns."
>
> *Discuss how well reasoned you find this argument. In your discussion be sure to analyze the line of reasoning and the use of evidence in the argument. For example, you may need to consider what questionable assumptions underlie the thinking and what alternative explanations or counterexamples might weaken the conclusion. You can also discuss what sort of evidence would strengthen or refute the argument, what changes in the argument would make it more logically sound, and what, if anything, would help you better evaluate its conclusion.*

Understand the argument

A spokesperson for Synthetic Farm Products claims that farmers should switch back to synthetic farming, despite the costs required for switching. He bases the claim on the fact that organic farming is economically unviable because organic crop yields were lower last year. He argues that while there would be a loss of the money invested in buying organic farming equipment, if farmers continue organic farming and do not switch back to synthetic farming, the losses from the continued lower yields would be a much bigger issue.

Faulty assumptions

- The selling price of both synthetic crops and organic crops are not significantly different

- Lower yields are significant enough to justify switching to synthetic crops

- Synthetic crop yields would not have been affected by factors that led to lower organic crop yields

- Organic crop yields would continue to be lower for the next few years at least

Missing evidence

- Data about the market price fetched by both organic and synthetic crops to compare price differences

- Details about how much lower the yield of organic crops was compared to a analogous synthetic crop yield

- Specifics about what caused the lower crop yields in organic farming and whether it would affect synthetic crops too

- Predictions and trends of estimated organic crop yields for the next few years

Counter-examples

- What if organic crops fetch much higher prices in the market?

- What if the organic crop yields are marginally lower and the lower yields are offset by the higher prices fetched by the organic crops?

- What if factors that reduced the organic crop yields would affect the synthetic crop yields similarly?

- What if the lower organic crop yields are temporary and eventually will be much higher than synthetic crop yields?

The essay

A spokesperson for Synthetic Farm Products claims that farmers should switch back to synthetic farming. His claim is based on numerous pieces of evidence provided in his argument. While the claim seems solid upon initial reading, a more detailed analysis reveals that several key facts are missing, leaving an incomplete picture full of assumptions.

To begin with, the primary support used by the spokesperson to advocate that farmers switch back to synthetic farming is that organic crop yields were lower last year. Many specifics are needed to evaluate whether this piece of support does the job it is intended to. A major piece of data needed is whether the lower organic crop yields have translated into lower profits for the farmers. For all we know, organic crops and related products fetch higher prices in the market, creating a bigger profit margin that even with lower yields can mean higher profits than earned with synthetic crops. Another piece of the puzzle needed to understand the impact of lower organic crop yields is the factors that caused them and whether those factors would have affected synthetic crop yields, too. If synthetic crops are just as likely to be affected, then switching to synthetic farming does not make any sense whatsoever. Also, the term "lower yields" is a bit ambiguous. Lower yields can still mean higher than synthetic crop yields, or can mean slightly lower but not necessarily low enough to switch to synthetic farming. Without all these necessary facts, determining the relevance of the support that organic crop yields were lower this year is impossible.

Another flaw in the argument is the spokesperson's direct assumption that the organic crop yields will continue to be lower. It is this assumption that he uses to suggest that it is far more economical to bear losses on the money spent on equipment for organic farming than endure continuing losses on lower crop yields in the coming year. Not a shred of proof has been furnished by the spokesperson to buttress his assumption that organic crop yields will continue to be lower in the coming years. Had he ascertained the specific factors that lowered organic crop yields and determined that those factors will continue in the future and cannot be dealt with, and that those factors will not affect crops in synthetic farming, his claim about economic feasibility would be more acceptable.

To conclude, the spokesperson relies on partial evidence and faulty assumptions in making his recommendations. Had he provided the complete picture, supported by relevant facts and figures, his claim would have been far stronger than it is now.

4.19 Essay 19 (Fern Valley University)

> *The following appeared as part of a recommendation from the financial planning office to the administration of Fern Valley University.*
>
> "In the past few years, Fern Valley University has suffered from a decline in both enrollments and admissions applications. The reason can be discovered from our students, who most often cite poor teaching and inadequate library resources as their chief sources of dissatisfaction with Fern Valley. Therefore, in order to increase the number of students attending our university, and hence to regain our position as the most prestigious university in the greater Fern Valley metropolitan area, it is necessary to initiate a fund-raising campaign among the alumni that will enable us to expand the range of subjects we teach and to increase the size of our library facilities."
>
> *Discuss how well reasoned you find this argument. In your discussion be sure to analyze the line of reasoning and the use of evidence in the argument. For example, you may need to consider what questionable assumptions underlie the thinking and what alternative explanations or counterexamples might weaken the conclusion. You can also discuss what sort of evidence would strengthen or refute the argument, what changes in the argument would make it more logically sound, and what, if anything, would help you better evaluate its conclusion.*

Understand the argument

The financial planning office of Fern Valley University recommends that the university raise funds from among the alumni to expand the range of subjects taught at the university and increase the size of library facilities, all to increase the number of students attending the university and improve its reputation. This recommendation is in response to the fact that there has been a decline in enrollments and admissions applications at Fern Valley University for the last few years. The department feels that the reason for this decline is that some students have been dissatisfied with the quality of teaching and library facilities at the school.

Faulty assumptions

- Poor teaching is connected to the range of subjects taught

- The students citing these reasons are representative of the other students in general

- No other factor has contributed significantly to the decline in enrollments or admissions applications

- No other factor is significantly responsible for the dissatisfaction expressed by students

Missing evidence

- Proof that the quality of teaching is directly related to the range of subjects taught

- Data on the students who cited the mentioned reasons

- Details about other possible factors that can affect enrollments or admissions applications

- Specifics about other factors that can cause dissatisfaction in students

Counter-examples

- What if quality of teaching is not significantly affected by the range of subjects but by some other factor?

- What if only a small portion of students are dissatisfied with the quality of teaching and library facilities while the majority are quite satisfied with these things?

- What if some other factor has led to the decline in enrollments and admissions applications?

- What if some other factor has caused dissatisfaction in students?

The essay

The financial planning office of Fern Valley University suggests that a fundraising campaign be initiated in order to increase the range of subjects taught at the university and to expand library facilities. The goal is mainly to halt the declining number of students and admissions by addressing these two issues. While the suggestion seems valid initially, a deeper investigation reveals that key facts are missing and important questions are unanswered, leaving the claim dubious.

To begin with, the department recommends that to remedy the declining number of students, the university should expand the range of subjects and improve library facilities. While both tasks are important and admirable goals in general, the department's reason for these goals is that students expressed dissatisfaction with the teaching and library facilities. Two questions beg to be answered before this suggestion can be evaluated. Are the students who cite dissatisfaction representative of all the students in general? If they are not, this move will not necessarily help to increase the number of students because it would appear that some other factor is responsible for the declining number. The second question that comes to mind is that even if the students are representative of all Fern Valley University students in general, how exactly is poor teaching connected to the range of subjects? If poor teaching is indeed the reason for the dissatisfaction and ultimately for the declining number of students, then the resolution would be to improve the quality of teaching, possibly by improving the curriculum, the manner in which it is taught, and the training of the teachers. Simply expanding the range of subjects taught will not affect the quality of teaching.

What the department should do is determine all the possible factors that might have resulted in the declining number of students and admissions, factors such as more and better universities, negative feedback from students, a booming job market, etc. When such factors are determined, then a proper course of measure should be charted to deal with those issues. Additionally, the department should also ascertain whether the students who express dissatisfaction speak for the majority. If they do, then measures should be taken to improve the quality of teaching and the library facilities. Finally, as a natural progression, the range of subjects should be expanded and library facilities improved after conducting a thorough survey of students and the market to determine the specifics of what subjects and what facilities would be best added.

To conclude, to simply assume that students expressing dissatisfaction is the primary reason for the declining number of students without specifically ascertaining so is illogical. Further, to use those assumptions and provide a cosmetic solution invites further trouble. Thus, the department should refrain from reactionary measures and take into account the aspects discussed above, after which the recommendation will be more sound and logical.

4.20 Essay 20 (Sacchar's trade deficit)

> *The following appeared as part of an article in a weekly newsmagazine.*
>
> "The country of Sacchar can best solve its current trade deficit problem by lowering the price of sugar, its primary export. Such an action would make Sacchar better able to compete for markets with other sugar exporting countries. The sale of Sacchar's sugar abroad would increase, and this increase would substantially reduce Sacchar's trade deficit."
>
> *Discuss how well reasoned you find this argument. In your discussion be sure to analyze the line of reasoning and the use of evidence in the argument. For example, you may need to consider what questionable assumptions underlie the thinking and what alternative explanations or counterexamples might weaken the conclusion. You can also discuss what sort of evidence would strengthen or refute the argument, what changes in the argument would make it more logically sound, and what, if anything, would help you better evaluate its conclusion.*

Understand the argument

An article claims that to reduce Sacchar's trade deficit, the country needs to increase the sale of Sacchar's sugar abroad. Sugar is the primary export of that country. When prices are lowered, Sacchar would be a better competitor, thereby increasing its exports, earning more foreign currency, and lowering its trade deficit.

Faulty assumptions

· Sacchar's competitors would not also lower the price of sugar to remain competitive

· Price is one of most significant determinants in the purchase of sugar; other factors such as quality, taste, etc. do not have a considerable impact

· Sacchar has the potential to meet raised demands for sugar without substantial investment in production

Missing evidence

· Specifics about Sacchar's competitors and whether they would lower their prices in response to Sacchar's move

· Details about factors considered by sugar importing countries that determine the purchase of sugar

· Data about Sacchar's current sugar-production capacity and whether it is capable of meeting increased demands generated by lowered prices

Counter-examples

· What if Sacchar's competitors lower their prices in response to Sacchar's move?

- What if price is only one of the many important factors considered by sugar importing countries, in addition to quality and taste?

- What if Sacchar's current sugar-production capacity is incapable of meeting increased demand and needs substantial investment to scale production up?

The essay

In a weekly newsmagazine, an article claims that the best way that Sacchar can deal with its trade deficit is by lowering the price of sugar. A couple of reasons have been cited by the article for this recommendation. While the claim seems like an easy quick-fix solution, detailed analysis will show that it assumes too much and provides too little evidence for it.

The primary issue with the proposition is its reliance on the assumption that making a move to grab a bigger portion of the market by lowering sugar prices would not invite competitors to do the same. What if the competitors, who want their own market share, also lower the price of sugar? The only thing this move would then achieve is a possible price war that would bring the price of sugar down to a bare minimum, profiting none and hurting all. A second assumption made in stating that lowering the price would necessarily increase the demand is that price is the only significant factor, and that other possible factors such as taste, quality, etc. have no impact whatsoever on the decision to purchase sugar. Price, albeit an important factor, is not the only thing that drives demand. Many aspects are factored into demand, ranging from the essentials such as price to the intangibles such as consumer perception. Simply relying on a price cut to trigger substantial demand is too risky, especially since it's a double-edged sword. While lowering the price might increases demand, and therefore sales, is Sacchar even capable of meeting increased demand? If that country's production capacity has already been optimized, scaling up would be difficult, time-consuming, and need great infusions of capital. Is the country of Sacchar prepared to do what might be necessary? Without evaluating this factor, lowering the price of sugar is illogical.

What the country should do is analyze its trade deficit to pinpoint wasteful expenditure. Trade deficits cannot be lowered simply by anticipating an increase in exports by lowering the price of the major exported product. Trade deficit is a complex issue that should be dealt with using a multi-pronged approach: curbing imports, increasing exports, and cutting out wasteful government expenditure. Further, before trying to boost exports by cutting prices, proper evaluation of possible measures by competitors and of production capacity should be conducted.

To conclude, acting upon the claim given in the article would be impossible because it is a hastily constructed, ill-supported and one-dimensional suggestion. Had the article taken into consideration the points discussed herein, the claim would have carried far more weight and sounded much more logical.

4.21   Essay 21 (Residential building permits)

> *The following appeared in a research paper written for an introductory economics course:*
>
> "For the past century, an increase in the number of residential building permits issued per month in a particular region has been a reliable indicator of coming improvements to that region's economy. If the monthly number of residential building permits issued rises consistently for a few months, the local unemployment rate almost always falls and economic production increases. This well-established connection reveals an effective method by which a regional government can end a local economic downturn: relax regulations governing all construction so that many more building permits can be issued."
>
> *Discuss how well reasoned you find this argument. In your discussion be sure to analyze the line of reasoning and the use of evidence in the argument. For example, you may need to consider what questionable assumptions underlie the thinking and what alternative explanations or counterexamples might weaken the conclusion. You can also discuss what sort of evidence would strengthen or refute the argument, what changes in the argument would make it more logically sound, and what, if anything, would help you better evaluate its conclusion.*

Understand the argument

The research paper recommends a measure that a regional government can take to end a local economic downturn. The paper recommends relaxing regulations governing all construction so that many more building permits can be issued. Based on a particular study, this would reduce local unemployment rates and increase production. The study, based on a particular region, found that an increase in the number of residential building permits issued per month is a reliable indicator of coming improvements in that region's economy.

Faulty assumptions

- There were no other elements which led to economic growth

- Currently, construction norms are restrictive and have scope for being relaxed further without an adverse impact on resilience of the structure and safety of the inhabitants

- The region is not already saturated with buildings and has scope for new constructions

- There will be demand for new buildings and there is not already an excess supply of properties

- What was true in that particular location and century will hold true everywhere and in the future

Missing evidence

- Proof that there is scope for more building constructions in this region and there is a demand for building and building permits

- Proof that the current construction norms are excessively restrictive and relaxing them will not lead to quality and safety issues

- Evidence that the region and the time period which was subject of the study is representative of all other regions and time periods

Counter-examples

- What if relaxing construction norms leads to poor construction quality that cannot withstand wear and tear, causes harm to inhabitants or incurs higher maintenance costs and thus has an adverse impact on the economy rather than a positive one?

- What if relaxing construction norms does not lead to increase in building permits issued?

- What if there is no demand for new buildings or already an oversupply of new buildings?

- What if there are other more effective ways of stimulating the economy which have been overlooked because the study has focused only on one indicator and missed more pivotal ones?

- What if the time and place of the study were unique and cannot be generalized to other times and places?

The essay

A research study proffers that the number of residential permits issued per month is a reliable indicator of the coming improvements to the economy. The study is based on statistics from a particular region over a century. It recommends relaxing construction norms to stimulate and overturn a downward economic spiral. The argument is too particularistic, does not take into account whether that study can be generalized to other times and regions, jumps to conclusions, ignores other factors that could be the reason for the stated outcome, and fails to consider any negative implications of its suggestions.

First, in a complex economic environment, which is also affected by various other factors such as politics, isolating one factor as a contributing factor may be insufficient, incomplete or even completely misleading. The study does not take into account other leading, lagging and co-incidental indicators or place the indicator of "issuance of building permits" within a holistic perspective. Although the number of building permits maybe one reliable indicator of future growth, as put forth by the study, it may not be the factor responsible for stimulating growth. It is possible that the economy growth was precipitated by a change in some government policy or due to industrial growth. Also the conditions prevalent during that time and place might be unique and any conclusion that may be valid there may not be so when generalized to other time, place and economies. Because other factors that could be pivotal to economic growth in that time period and place have not been discussed or delineated, and no discussion is made about the conditions where this generalization would work, the argument makes a recommendation which is tenuous and merits further qualifications.

Second, even if the conclusions of the study were reliable and the findings could be generalized to a particular time and place, the overly broad recommendations of merely relaxing the construction norms may have insidious effects on the economy. Assuming that there is demand for new construction and not an already excess supply of buildings, what if relaxing construction norms leads to unstable structures ad poor quality construction both of which could cause damage to life and property at the worst and increase in maintenance costs at the least? What would be the impact on the economy or even confidence of people in the government's ability to regulate the economy and govern its people? At the worst it could lead to total anarchy and an uprising and at the least it could undermine confidence in the government and economy, inadvertently leading to a downward economic spiral since a precarious political environment can seldom provide a thriving ground for the economy. Finally, the role of the government is not only to stimulate the economy but also to safeguard its people and their long-term interests.

If the study considers other political and economic factors playing out during that time at that place and places economic growth within a more holistic perspective and provides a convincing conclusion for what measures can be taken under which conditions to stimulate the economy at which stage, it would be more helpful for policy and decision makers.

4.22   Essay 22 (Local clothing stores)

The following appeared as part of a recommendation from the business manager of a department store:

"Local clothing stores reported that their profits decreased, on average, for the three-month period between August 1 and October 31. Stores that sell products for the home reported that, on average, their profits increased during this same period. Clearly, consumers are choosing to buy products for their homes instead of clothing. To take advantage of this trend, we should reduce the size of our clothing departments and enlarge our home furnishings and household products departments."

Discuss how well reasoned you find this argument. In your discussion be sure to analyze the line of reasoning and the use of evidence in the argument. For example, you may need to consider what questionable assumptions underlie the thinking and what alternative explanations or counterexamples might weaken the conclusion. You can also discuss what sort of evidence would strengthen or refute the argument, what changes in the argument would make it more logically sound, and what, if anything, would help you better evaluate its conclusion.

Understand the argument

A department store manager recommends that the store reduce the size of its clothing departments and enlarge its household products departments. The recommendation is based on the conclusion that there is a change in purchase trends in favor of household products and against clothing. This conclusion is based on the following: while local clothing stores reported an average reduction in profits for a three-month period of 1 August to 31 October, home product stores reported an average increase in profits.

Faulty assumptions

- Data over a three-month period is indicative of future performance

- There are no extremes skewing the value of the average

- Increase in profits is due to increase in sales and not due to reduction in costs

- The clothing and home goods businesses are not seasonal in nature and sales are uniformly spread throughout the year

- The household products stores are not durables or long-term purchases and will have to be replaced in the short-term

Missing evidence

- Evidence that the household goods stores increased sales and not reduced costs to achieve increase in profits and vice-versa for clothing stores

- Data to determine that the average is not skewed because of abnormal figures by a few stores in either category – household goods and clothing

· Evidence that these figures are not indicative of the seasonal nature of the respective businesses

Counter-examples

· What if the three-month period represents an anomaly or a seasonal bias rather than a new trend?

· What if the average figure is completely misleading because it includes online stores that have lower costs and, thus, more profits?

· What if the store in question is well-known for its clothing line and not household goods?

· What if the home furnishings and household goods businesses made more sales during this period because it is the period when people move into new homes/rented apartments and will not make such purchases again for a long time?

· What if the aforesaid period represents a peak season for home goods and a trough for clothing rather than a continuing trend?

The essay

A department store business manager recommends a resizing of two of the store's departments. This recommendation follows a conclusion that there is a shift in purchase trends favorable towards household furnishings and home goods and one that is unfavorable towards clothes. This conclusion is based on average profit figures of a three-month period 1 August to 31 October; there was an increase in average profits for home goods and decrease in average profits for clothing. The argument is based on insufficient data, faulty conclusions, and hasty recommendations.

The entire premise of the argument is based on the average profit figures for a three-month period. The reasoning is faulty on multiple levels. First, the average is not a representative number. An average can be easily skewed by the presence of even one anomaly or extreme high or low value and thus is not a reliable representation of the whole. Second, the data is about profits and the conclusion is about customer purchases or sales or revenues. Profits are not a function of merely the revenue but also the cost. So the sales or revenue numbers are needed to arrive at a logical conclusion about customer purchases. Third, this particular three-month period is not sufficient to predict an annual or month-on-month trend. This period could be a deviation from the annual figures and even represent a seasonal trend in these businesses.

Further, a comparison is being made between two very different product categories without understanding the nature of businesses and customer trends in each. The two could be very different categories but are being pitched as competing product categories. Perhaps they could act as complementary product categories and provide a reasonable hedge against any seasonal variations in sales in each. The argument also fails to take into account the fact that home furnishings and home products are more durable than clothing in general and long-term purchases for many people, whereas clothing is a necessity and frequency of purchase is perhaps much more than home products. Also, the argument needs to consider the sales figures and profit margins associated with its own store, since this store might have more clientele for one category rather than the other, notwithstanding general trends.

In conclusion, the argument's central premise needs to be investigated further with relevant and representative data. Further, attention needs to be paid that relevant comparisons are made rather than ad-hoc ones. The case for greater profits can be made stronger by cost-control measures such as closely monitoring and managing the inventories and sales-boosting measures such as increasing footfalls through sales, stimulating customer interest through new product lines, and even exploring alternative means of expansion by increasing their on-line presence.

4.23 Essay 23 (Petty vandalism vs Crime)

> *The following appeared in a letter to the editor of a regional newspaper:*
>
> "In response to petitions from the many farmers and rural landowners throughout our region, the legislature has spent valuable time and effort enacting severe laws to deter motorists from picking fruit off the trees, trampling through the fields, and stealing samples of foliage. But how can our local lawmakers occupy themselves with such petty vandalism when crime and violence plague the nation's cities? The fate of apples and leaves is simply too trivial to merit their attention."
>
> *Discuss how well reasoned you find this argument. In your discussion be sure to analyze the line of reasoning and the use of evidence in the argument. For example, you may need to consider what questionable assumptions underlie the thinking and what alternative explanations or counterexamples might weaken the conclusion. You can also discuss what sort of evidence would strengthen or refute the argument, what changes in the argument would make it more logically sound, and what, if anything, would help you better evaluate its conclusion.*

Understand the argument

In a letter to the editor, citizen expresses his or her concern that the local lawmakers are wasting their time and energy over trivial matters while crime and violence are rampant in the cities. The trivial matter in question is the enactment of strict laws which protect farmers and rural landowners from vandalism and theft such as picking fruit off trees, trampling through the fields, and stealing samples of foliage. The new laws by the legislature are in response to petitions from the farmers and rural landowners throughout the region.

Faulty assumptions

- Lawmakers should concern themselves only with serious crimes and not petty ones

- Petty crimes are not indicators of serious crimes

- Lawmakers have not already put in place adequate laws to deter crimes and violence

- The crimes and violence in the cities is due to insufficient laws and not a result of other issues such as law enforcement or unemployment

Missing evidence

- Evidence that laws regarding serious crimes are not already in place

- Evidence that the crimes in the cities is due to inadequate laws rather than unemployment or lapses in law enforcement

- Data about the actual number of petty crimes and serious crimes as well as any correlation between them

Counter-examples

- What if a rise in petty crimes has been an indicator of rise in serious crimes?

- What if controlling petty crimes can mitigate trends in serious crimes?

- What if the country consists of a majority of rural population and a minority of urban population?

- What if instances of petty crimes are much greater than those of serious crimes?

- What if adequate legislation for serious crimes is already in place?

The essay

A letter to the editor in a regional newspaper raises a concern that the lawmakers are abdicating their duties by directing an inordinate amount of time and effort in formulating legislature to deter petty crimes affecting farmers and rural landowners in rural areas at the expense of serious crimes and violence plaguing the country's cities. This argument lacks data about the frequency of the types of crimes, data about distribution of population between urban and rural areas, examination of any correlation between petty and serious crimes, and the existing legislation with respect to serious crimes.

The argument, although very impassioned, makes several unexamined assumptions and lacks support for its claims. Recent legislation on petty thefts and vandalism (picking fruit off the trees, trampling through the fields, and stealing samples of foliage) affecting farmers has been highlighted as trivial. The argument fails to consider that lawmakers have a responsibility towards all citizens, including rural population, and not just towards urban residents. The argument fails to consider the distribution of population among rural and urban areas. If the rural areas have the majority of the population and urban the minority, it is incumbent on the legislature to address the issues that affect a majority of the population. What is also not considered is the possibility that a surge in petty crimes might actually lead to an increase in serious crimes by perpetuating economic losses for the rural population, thereby leading to a trickle-down effect in the urban areas where it snowballs into violence and serious crimes.

The writer of the letter also fails to consider the current legislation on serious crimes and violence. It is possible that the real reasons for serious crimes in urban areas lies elsewhere, such as unemployment, overpopulation, political motivations, or lack of adequate implementation measures and law enforcement personnel, and has nothing to do with inadequate legislation. Further, the writer fails to consider the possibility that just because there is focus on legislation deterring petty crimes does not automatically mean that lawmakers are ignoring serious crimes and violence. Perhaps, they are paying lots of attention to serious crimes but only their efforts towards prevention of petty crimes is being highlighted by the media. Or perhaps it is taking longer to formulate legislation pertaining to serious crimes because it requires more deliberation and longer research and is currently in progress, while legislation pertaining to petty crimes could be rolled out much more quickly.

To sum up, the letter to the editor seems like it is driven more by emotions than by evidence and lacks statistics to appraise whether the legislature is up to the mark or is failing in its duties towards the citizens.

4.24 Essay 24 (Retail spaces in Palm Grove)

> *The following appeared in a letter from a part-owner of a small retail clothing chain to her business partner:*
>
> "Commercial real estate prices have been rising steadily in the Sandida Heights neighborhood for several years, while the prices in the adjacent neighborhood of Palm Grove have remained the same. It seems obvious, then, that a retail space in Sandida Heights must now be much more expensive than a similar space in Palm Grove, which was not the case several years ago. So, it appears that retail spaces in Sandida Heights are now overpriced relative to those in Palm Grove. Therefore, it would be in our financial interest to purchase a retail space in Palm Grove rather than in Sandida Heights."
>
> *Discuss how well reasoned you find this argument. In your discussion be sure to analyze the line of reasoning and the use of evidence in the argument. For example, you may need to consider what questionable assumptions underlie the thinking and what alternative explanations or counterexamples might weaken the conclusion. You can also discuss what sort of evidence would strengthen or refute the argument, what changes in the argument would make it more logically sound, and what, if anything, would help you better evaluate its conclusion.*

Understand the argument

A part-owner of a small retail clothing chain raises a concern about the rising commercial real estate prices in the Sandida Heights neighborhood where the store is located. Citing the steady real estate prices in the adjacent neighborhood of Palm Grove, the argument makes a case for relocating to the reasonably priced neighborhood Palm Grove. The business partner making the argument does so in accordance with the financial interests of the business.

Faulty assumptions

·   Financial interests of a business are commensurate with merely the costs rather than profits or revenues

·   There will be an appropriate property available for sale at Palm Grove

·   Shifting to Palm Grove will not take away the current established client base at Sandida Heights and the revenue after relocating to Palm Grove will be unaffected

·   Palm Grove residents have the same demographics as those of Sandida Heights

·   Palm Grove does not have fierce competition for their clothing business

Missing evidence

·   Evidence that real estate prices at Sandida Heights will not fall in the future, thus hurting the financial interests of the business

·   Evidence that sales/revenue will not be adversely affected at the new location

- Data that the new neighbourhood is similar in terms of its demographics of the old neighbourhood and does not already have fierce competition

- Data about whether currently the property is rented or owned and exactly what would be the relocation's impact on the bottom line

Counter-examples

- What if the rise in prices in the current neighbourhood is because of an increase in demand (a promising trend for any business)?

- What if the store already has an established client base in the current location?

- What if moving to a new neighbourhood will cause a loss in customer base?

- What if the new locality does not have adequate target customers of the clothing line that the store retails?

- What if the reason the commercial real estate is not going up at the neighbouring locality is that is not conducive to businesses due to perhaps vandalism?

The essay

The part-owner of a small retail clothing store proposes that the store be relocated from Sandida Heights, which is showing increase in prices, to Palm Grove, which has steady real estate prices. The case made is that of the financial interests of the business. The recommendation involves purchasing a retail property at Palm Grove. To evaluate this argument, more details are required with respect to the current financial situation of the store, including whether it is being rented currently or is self-owned, demographic details of their clientele, and any evaluation of how the relocation will impact not just their costs but also their revenues.

First, more details are required about the current situation of the business. Details would include whether the retail space at Sandida Heights is self-owned or rented. If it is self-owned, the business will perhaps require a buyer for the property before a new property can be purchased at Palm Grove. If it is rented, then how long the lease agreement is needs to be looked into. If the lease is valid for next several years and the exit clause with respect to the lease is prohibitive then it might not be a good idea financially to relocate at this time. And by the time the lease ends in some distant future, the scenario about property rates might have changed drastically and will have to be given a fresh look. Also, the plan is also incumbent upon whether an appropriate commercial retail space is available for sale at Palm Grove.

Further, even if it is established that the property prices are better and it is feasible to move to Palm Grove, what needs to be evaluated is whether the overall profits will increase. What if, although the bottom line improves, the topline reduces and overall there is an adverse impact on the total profits of the store? The sales could be adversely affected due to factors such as loss of current client base, inadequate numbers of relevant demographics of Palm Grove residents, or fierce existing competition at Palm Grove? What if the store is carrying luxury brands, which has the relevant clientele at Sandida Heights but not at Palm Grove?

In conclusion, although at first glance the argument to purchase a property at the neighboring Palm Grove locality sounds convincing on account of differences in property rates, the argument requires further proof and examination of assumptions to evaluate whether it is a tenable plan and will lead to the desired goal of furthering financial interests.

4.25 Essay 25 (demand for highly skilled workers)

> *The following appeared as part of an editorial in a campus newspaper:*
>
> "With an increasing demand for highly skilled workers, this nation will soon face a serious labor shortage. New positions in technical and professional occupations are increasing rapidly, while at the same time the total labor force is growing slowly. Moreover, the government is proposing to cut funds for aid to education in the near future."
>
> *Discuss how well reasoned you find this argument. In your discussion be sure to analyze the line of reasoning and the use of evidence in the argument. For example, you may need to consider what questionable assumptions underlie the thinking and what alternative explanations or counterexamples might weaken the conclusion. You can also discuss what sort of evidence would strengthen or refute the argument, what changes in the argument would make it more logically sound, and what, if anything, would help you better evaluate its conclusion.*

Understand the argument

An editorial in a campus newspaper predicts that there will be an acute shortage of highly skilled workers. The premise of the argument is that there is a rapid increase in new positions in technical and professional occupations, but a relatively slower growth in labor force. The argument also states that the government proposal of reducing funds to aid education in the near future would exacerbate the situation.

Faulty assumptions

- The current trend of rapid increase in positions and slower increase in total labor force will continue in the future

- The slow increase in the total labor force is commensurate with a slow increase in the skilled labor force

- Government always implements its proposals

- The professional and skilled education and training sector is largely government funded

- The skills gap in the country cannot be bridged by hiring skilled professionals from other countries

Missing evidence

- Evidence that the current trend is indicative of the future trend

- Evidence that the private education and training sector cannot contribute towards the training of skilled workers

- Evidence that currently the government is funding the highly skilled trainings in the country and not just the primary and secondary education sectors.

Counter-examples

· What if the current trend is temporary and will change in the future?

· What if government does not implement its proposal?

· What if the government funding has no impact on the education and training of skilled workers?

· What if there is a large pool of expatriate candidates available to be tapped into for any skill shortages that might arise?

· What if even if the number of skilled workers in the country were to increase, they would not remain in the country and would leave the country for better opportunities?

The essay

An editorial in the campus newspaper raises a concern that two concomitant trends will create an acute shortage of skilled workers in the future. One trend is that of rapid increase in new positions in technical and professional occupations and the other trend is that of the total labor force growing at a slow rate. The argument states that another factor exacerbating the situation is a recent proposal by the government to reduce subsidizations for education in the near future. This argument has several unexamined assumptions and lacks sufficient evidence and is hence too perfunctory to merit any attention to the alarm it raises.

To begin, the argument needs to do a trend analysis and forecasting taking into account changes in the micro and macro environments to accurately determine whether the existing trends will continue in the future. The rapid increase in new positions in technical and professional occupations could be a temporary rather than enduring situation. Further, even if there was a lacuna in the supply, it could perhaps easily be remedied by seeking qualified professionals from other countries. Further, the slow increase in total labor force does not specify the trend with respect to skilled worker. It is possible that even if there is a slow increase in the total labor force, the supply of skilled workers could actually be increasing or just ample and the slow increase could actually be due to slow increase in unskilled labor.

Even if the number of skilled workers were to increase, it may not mean that they would not choose to work abroad; in such a situation, even if the government continues subsidizing education, the benefits would not be available for the home country. That the government has proposed something does not automatically translate into its implementation; there is many a gap between the cup and the lip, especially in the case of government proposals. Even if the government were to carry out its proposal to reduce funding to aid education, further data is required to analyze the policy's impact. In case, currently, the government subsidy to professional and trade schools is negligible, and this sector is largely privately funded, then the policy would have no impact on the availability of skilled labor.

To conclude, in the current form, the argument is tenuous. The author could strengthen the argument with further analysis of the trends, more data, and examination of its assumptions to validate whether the concern about skilled labor shortage raised by it is valid.

4.26   Essay 26 (A bridge on the Styx River)

> *The following appeared as part of a memorandum from a government agency:*
>
> "Given the limited funding available for the building and repair of roads and bridges, the government should not spend any money this year on fixing the bridge that crosses the Styx River. This bridge is located near a city with a weakening economy, so it is not as important as other bridges; moreover, the city population is small and thus unlikely to contribute a significant enough tax revenue to justify the effort of fixing the bridge."
>
> *Discuss how well reasoned you find this argument. In your discussion be sure to analyze the line of reasoning and the use of evidence in the argument. For example, you may need to consider what questionable assumptions underlie the thinking and what alternative explanations or counterexamples might weaken the conclusion. You can also discuss what sort of evidence would strengthen or refute the argument, what changes in the argument would make it more logically sound, and what, if anything, would help you better evaluate its conclusion.*

Understand the argument

A government memorandum proposes that since limited amount of funding is available for the building and repair of roads and bridges, the government should not fund the repair of the Styx River Bridge. The reasoning for this recommendation is that the surrounding economy is unlikely to contribute much to the tax revenues because of small size of the population and weakening economy of the nearby city.

Faulty assumptions

- Government funding should be used primarily for tax-generating activities

- Safety of citizens is not the government's role

- The population size is commensurate with taxable incomes

- The government cannot find private enterprises to fund the repair of the bridge

Missing evidence

- Evidence that the government will not be sued in the case of damage to life or goods, leading to a dent in its coffers

- Evidence that the small population cannot generate disproportionately large tax revenues

- Evidence that the government's sole guiding policy for any decision should be generation of tax revenues rather than ensuring the welfare of its citizens

- Evidence that the weakening economy is not going to be strong in the future

- Evidence that the bridge will not be a contribution to strengthening the economy by facilitating exchange of goods and services

Counter-examples

- What if any untoward situation such as collapse of bridge will incur the government much greater costs in terms of negligence lawsuits or rebuilding the bridge or even losing electorate confidence?

- What if the nearby city has only a temporary weakening of economy and will thrive soon?

- What if the government could come up with alternative means of funding the construction and repairs of bridges, including local or national business sponsors?

The essay

A memorandum from a government agency recommends not spending any money on the repairs of the Styx River. The reasoning provided for this recommendation is as follows: there is shortage of funds available for building and repair of roads and bridges; and since the bridge is located near a city that has a weakening economy and a small population, it is unlikely to generate significant tax revenues. The argument is based on faulty assumption, inept reasoning, and makes recommendations that must be scrutinized further before they are paid any heed to.

The central premise of the argument is tenuous and, perhaps, even dangerous to the welfare of a nation that delegates its care to the government it elects. The reasoning that any expenditure needs to be justified by the revenue it will generate is inapplicable when applied to the government, since the sole aim of the government is not tax revenue generation. Is the government a profit-making enterprise which must base all its decisions on the balance sheet relegating to secondary importance the safety and welfare of its citizens? Such reasoning is blasphemous for a government agency and dangerous for the society as a whole.

Further, considering the fact that managing a healthy balance-sheet is one of the secondary functions of a responsible government, let us evaluate the evidence for the supposed claim that the bridge would be an unwise expenditure financially. The bridge connects a city with a weakening economy. We need further evidence in terms of numbers and also a trend across time to understand the extent and impact of this "weakening." What if the city's economy was doing extremely well before and now is doing moderately well? If that were true, it would still be a strong economy. What if the weakening was just a blip in an otherwise strong growth trend? Further, merely because the city's population is small does not automatically mean that tax revenues generated from there would be less. What if the small population consists of extremely rich people? In which case, the amounts of revenues generated would be humungous and any neglect would hurt the city coffers. Further, what if the bridge due to want of repairs were to collapse causing damage to life and property? In that case, the government would become vulnerable to negligence lawsuits and even lower electorate confidence, hurting voter sentiments.

In sum, a parochial outlook is not befitting a government which needs to think from a larger perspective then merely financial perspective. Further, more creative solutions can be generated such as allowing a local business to sponsor the repairs for the bridge.

4.27   Essay 27 (Purchase manager to sales manager)

> *The following appeared in a report presented for discussion at a meeting of the directors of a company that manufactures parts for heavy machinery:*
>
> "The falling revenues that the company is experiencing coincide with delays in manufacturing. These delays, in turn, are due in large part to poor planning in purchasing metals. Consider further that the manager of the department that handles purchasing of raw materials has an excellent background in general business, psychology, and sociology, but knows little about the properties of metals. The company should, therefore, move the purchasing manager to the sales department and bring in a scientist from the research division to be manager of the purchasing department."
>
> *Discuss how well reasoned you find this argument. In your discussion be sure to analyze the line of reasoning and the use of evidence in the argument. For example, you may need to consider what questionable assumptions underlie the thinking and what alternative explanations or counterexamples might weaken the conclusion. You can also discuss what sort of evidence would strengthen or refute the argument, what changes in the argument would make it more logically sound, and what, if anything, would help you better evaluate its conclusion.*

Understand the argument

The report states that the revenues of a manufacturing company are decreasing and delves into the causes for the same. It claims that the declining revenues of the company accompany delays in manufacturing, implying that the former is caused by the latter. The report cites inefficient planning by the purchasing manager to be responsible for the delays in manufacturing and the resultant slump in revenues. Though the report concedes that the manager possesses good business knowledge and is well-informed on general psychology and sociology, his lack of technical knowledge on properties of metals is identified as an impediment. To overcome this problem and consequently boost up revenues, the report suggests appointing a scientist from the research department as the new manager of the purchasing department and shifting the purchasing manager to the sales department.

Faulty assumptions

- Coincidence of declining revenues and delays in manufacturing imply a cause and effect relationship

- Delays caused in manufacturing can directly be attributed to the manager's performance

- Knowledge of metal properties is enough for proper planning for purchasing metals

- The purchasing manager can fit in the sales department without affecting the performance of either department

- There are no other factors that have caused the decline in revenues

- The scientist would have or develop knowledge of general business, psychology, and sociology

Missing evidence

- Proof that delay in manufacturing is responsible for decline in revenues

- Proof that poor planning in purchasing of metals is responsible for the delay in manufacturing and the manager is accountable for this poor planning

- Proof that it is the manager's lack of knowledge about metal properties that has caused poor planning and delays in manufacturing

- Proof that the scientist has the necessary general business, psychology, and sociology know-how

Counter-examples

- What if there is no direct cause and effect relationship between delays in manufacturing and declining revenues?

- What if there are some other factors that have caused a decline in revenues?

- What if the delays were in fact being caused due to lack of funds arising out of declining revenues in the first place?

- What if the manager does not fit in the sales department and sales decrease resulting in further declining revenues?

- What if the scientist lacks knowledge in general business, psychology and sociology which may also result in poor planning of purchasing metals?

The essay

A company operating in the business of manufacturing heavy machinery is experiencing declining revenues. The report tabled in a meeting of the directors draws a correlation between the declining revenues of the company and delays in manufacturing. The report further states that these delays are caused by poor planning on part of the purchasing manager. His lack of knowledge on metal properties is cited as a reason for his poor performance. The report suggests bringing in a scientist from the research department as a solution for the problem. It also suggests moving the purchasing manager to the sales department. The argument is riddled with numerous incorrect assumptions and suggests a solution without relying on substantial evidence to support it.

The first flaw in the argument sets in when the report assumes that two things happening at the same time necessarily have to have a cause and effect relationship. The report only states that delays in manufacturing and decline in revenues are happening at the same time. This doesn't mean that decline in revenues is due to the delays in manufacturing. The decline in revenues may be a result of other factors such as decline in sales, increased cost of raw materials, changed market conditions, etc. It is in fact possible that the delay in manufacturing is a result of lack of funds arising out of declining revenues. The second flaw in the argument is the assumption that the purchasing manager is solely responsible for the delays in manufacturing and none of the other employees or practices in the department can be responsible for this delay. Thirdly, the argument baselessly assumes that it is the manager's lack of knowledge on metal properties that has caused poor planning in purchasing metals and the subsequent delay. The report doesn't provide any evidence which can support the claim that one has to have proper knowledge of metal properties to make successful purchase decisions.

As a solution, the report suggests appointing a scientist from the research department as a manager of the purchasing department and the purchase manager to be moved to the sales department. This suggestion is highly questionable as it relies on many faulty assumptions. First, it fails to take into account the possibility that the scientist may not have the required business acumen to work successfully in the purchase department. The argument suggests that the former manager has excellent background in general business, psychology, and sociology, and it is not evident that the scientist possesses these qualities to run the purchasing activities efficiently. Secondly, the argument assumes that since the said person is a scientist, he/she ought to have knowledge on metal properties. Lastly, the argument doesn't consider the other repercussions that this move may have, such as – the former manager may not fit in the sales department and this may cause declines in the sales in turn resulting in declining revenues, the scientist's lack of general business knowledge may result in losses far greater than gains he may provide owing to his knowledge of metals, etc.

In order to address the problem of declining revenues, the directors of the company need to first assess the main reasons for this decline. Arriving at a solution is only possible when the right cause has been identified. After all the responsible factors have been identified, it pays to understand what corrective actions the company can take to remedy the situation. The directors need to assess if they can reduce production costs, increase sales and plug any knowledge gaps that its employees may have. Presently, the argument only looks at one cause, whose link to the problem itself is questionable, and goes on to delve on unimportant aspects to improve the situation.

4.28   Essay 28 (Cumquat cafee)

> *The following appeared as part of a campaign to sell advertising time on a local radio station to local businesses:*
>
> "The Cumquat cafee began advertising on our local radio station this year and was delighted to see its business increase by 10 percent over last year's totals. Their success shows you how you can use radio advertising to make your business more profitable."
>
> *Discuss how well reasoned you find this argument. In your discussion be sure to analyze the line of reasoning and the use of evidence in the argument. For example, you may need to consider what questionable assumptions underlie the thinking and what alternative explanations or counterexamples might weaken the conclusion. You can also discuss what sort of evidence would strengthen or refute the argument, what changes in the argument would make it more logically sound, and what, if anything, would help you better evaluate its conclusion.*

Understand the argument

A local radio station has claimed that The Cumquat cafee did better business as compared to last year's after it advertised itself on the radio station. Taking this success as a benchmark, the radio station invites other businesses to advertise themselves on the radio in order to fetch more business and rake in more money.

Faulty assumptions

- The 10% year on year increase in business is clearly due to advertising on the radio and no other factor is responsible for this

- The cafee either did not advertise itself in any other format or no such advertising had any contribution in the said success

- A formula that worked for one business will work for other businesses as well

- It is not natural for the cafee to achieve this yearly growth percentage otherwise

Missing evidence

- The increase in business for the cafee is actually due to advertising on the radio

- The cafee made no other efforts to increase sales which could have resulted in increasing profits

- All other businesses are similar in nature to that of the cafee and would also benefit from radio advertising, just as Cumquat cafee did

- Proof that the cafee never grew as much previously when it did not advertise on the radio

Counter-examples

- What if the cafee grew at a better rate last year, when it did not advertise on the radio?

- What if the cafee engaged in a lot of promotions through other media such as Television and Print?

- What if the radio audience is of a certain demographic who may not find the advertisements of other businesses relevant?

- What if the cafee grew at this rate due to normal increase in population, better purchasing power of customers, etc.?

The essay

The argument relates to a part of an advertising campaign by a local radio station. The radio station cites the example of one of its clients, The Cumquat cafee, which advertised on the radio station and experienced a 10% growth in its business over last year's. Alluding to the cafee's success, the radio claims that advertising your business on its channel would bring you better business and make you profitable. The argument is flawed in not considering any other factors that may have impacted the cafee success, or that radio advertising may not work for every other business in the same way as it did for the cafee.

To begin with, drawing the conclusion that Cumquat cafee's business growth can be ascribed to its advertisements on the radio is merely a claim that the radio station fails to substantiate. In the absence of any evidence that can link the cafee's growth with its decision to advertise on the radio, this claim becomes baseless. It may be possible that in the preceding year, the cafee undertook a host of measures to increase its sales, radio advertising being one. The growth, hence, could be a cumulative result of all such measures. Even if one admits that it was indeed the radio that steered the cafee to better business, it can't be concluded for certain that a similar success can be replicated for all other businesses that advertise on the radio. It may be possible that the other businesses do not lend themselves to such advertising and hence wouldn't reap profits.

Analyzing the argument further, one can uncover many other flaws. For one, a 10% increase over last year's total is an absolute number that cannot be understood to mean that the cafee had a successful year. It could have been possible that the cafee grew by, say, 20% the preceding year and its growth rate rather declined in the year in question. Secondly, it could have been possible that the cafee was anyways poised for this growth given, for example, the increasing purchasing power of the people in the area, the shutdown of the competing cafee, word of mouth publicity, opening of an educational institute nearby, etc. Lastly, generalizing one business's success to mean the success of the advertising medium as a whole is incorrect as the success of the former may be due to factors independent of the contribution of the latter. Hence, the local radio's assertion that advertising on its channel would lead to success for its clients is a claim that the businesses should take with a pinch of salt.

4.29   Essay 29 (Coffee vs Cola)

> *The following appeared as part of the business plan of an investment and financial consulting firm:*
>
> "Studies suggest that an average coffee drinker's consumption of coffee increases with age, from age 10 through age 60. Even after age 60, coffee consumption remains high. The average cola drinker's consumption of cola, however, declines with increasing age. Both of these trends have remained stable for the past 40 years. Given that the number of older adults will significantly increase as the population ages over the next 20 years, it follows that the demand for coffee will increase and the demand for cola will decrease during this period. We should, therefore, consider transferring our investments from Cola Loca to Early Bird Coffee."
>
> *Discuss how well reasoned you find this argument. In your discussion be sure to analyze the line of reasoning and the use of evidence in the argument. For example, you may need to consider what questionable assumptions underlie the thinking and what alternative explanations or counterexamples might weaken the conclusion. You can also discuss what sort of evidence would strengthen or refute the argument, what changes in the argument would make it more logically sound, and what, if anything, would help you better evaluate its conclusion.*

Understand the argument

An investment and financial consulting firm advises its clients to transfer their investments from cola to coffee companies as the demand for coffee would increase and that of cola would decrease in the near future. The firm draws its conclusions from the findings of certain studies that suggest that an average coffee drinker consumes increasingly more coffee during his lifetime while his cola-drinking counterpart's consumption decreases as he ages. This finding, coupled with the "fact" that the number of older adults will increase in the next twenty years, provides basis to the firm's conclusion.

Faulty assumptions

· Total absolute consumption of cola is less than that of coffee

· The growth rate of population is marginal

· The rate of increase and decrease of coffee and cola consumption for an average person over the years is the same

· Returns on investment are better for a firm with greater demand for a commodity when compared with a firm that has a lesser demand for its product

Missing evidence

· Proof that there wouldn't be any new young population added to the existing lot to make up for the increase in the aging population

- Proof that the total net consumption of cola is less than the total consumption of coffee

- Proof that the rate of decrease of cola consumption is not less than the rate of increase of coffee consumption

Counter-examples

- What if an average adult drinks more cola than coffee during his entire lifetime?

- What if there is a population explosion and the older adults are outnumbered by a younger population?

- What if the cola consumption decreases at a far lesser rate than the rate at which the coffee consumption increases?

- What if the cola companies still do better business than the coffee ones, despite relatively lower demands for cola?

The essay

An investment consulting firm dishes out advice to its clients to invest more in coffee companies vis-a-vis cola companies based on the conclusion that in the next 20 years, coffee demand would surpass cola demand. The firm draws this conclusion based on the findings of a study that states a general trend of increasing coffee consumption for an average person as he ages from 10 to 60 years and a corresponding decrease in cola consumption during the same time. The firm further presumes that in the next 20 years, the present population would age and outnumber the younger, cola drinking ones, and this would mean that the demand for coffee would be greater than that of cola. The investment firm overlooks several other aspects that can counteract this increased demand for coffee – natural population growth being the most obvious.

To understand the flaws in the argument, it's important to first understand what the research findings suggest and imply. It is stated that an average coffee drinker's coffee consumption increases with age – beginning from the age of 10 until 60. Similarly, for an average cola drinker, the cola consumption decreases with age. Now, this piece of information could mean anything in relation to absolute quantity of cola and coffee demanded. For example, for an average person, who drinks both cola and coffee, the cola consumption could be way greater than his coffee consumption, even though he may absolutely fall in line with the study's findings – that over the years, he would prefer coffee to cola. Further, even if the absolute consumption of coffee becomes greater than that of cola for an average person with age, the total consumption of cola may still be greater than that of coffee for the sheer number of youngsters in the population. Hence, the investment firm wrongly analyzes the report's findings in several ways to arrive at the given conclusion.

The firm commits its second blunder in assuming that over the next 20 years, the population would not grow significantly and the number of older adults would increase to a greater proportion, driving the demand for coffee. If the number of older adults would increase, assuming constant life expectancy, it is likely that this increase would be balanced out by the rise of young population. Hence, the expected increase in demand for coffee would be met by a corresponding or a greater increase in demand for cola too.

The investment firm should instead analyze the research findings further to know what the population breakup of the area is, how much is the decrease in cola consumption in relation to the increase in coffee consumption, what the returns on investment are for both cola and coffee companies, etc. Only when it investigates into all these angle would it be able to give sound investment advice to its clients.

4.30 Essay 30 (West Cambria ambulance service)

> *The following appeared in the editorial section of a West Cambria newspaper:*
>
> "A recent review of the West Cambria volunteer ambulance service revealed a longer average response time to accidents than was reported by a commercial ambulance squad located in East Cambria. In order to provide better patient care for accident victims and to raise revenue for our town by collecting service fees for ambulance use, we should disband our volunteer service and hire a commercial ambulance service."
>
> *Discuss how well reasoned you find this argument. In your discussion be sure to analyze the line of reasoning and the use of evidence in the argument. For example, you may need to consider what questionable assumptions underlie the thinking and what alternative explanations or counterexamples might weaken the conclusion. You can also discuss what sort of evidence would strengthen or refute the argument, what changes in the argument would make it more logically sound, and what, if anything, would help you better evaluate its conclusion.*

Understand the argument

A local newspaper from West Cambria has reported that the volunteer ambulance service of the region has had a longer average response time to accidents than that of the commercial ambulance service that operates in East Cambria. Comparing the two services, the editorial column suggests hiring a commercial ambulance service for the region so as to ensure better patient care and also rake in some money in the form of service fee that will add to the town's revenue. It also suggest discontinuing the volunteer ambulance service in favor of the commercial one.

Faulty assumptions

- Lower response time to accidents necessarily means better patient care

- The average response time of the volunteer ambulance service is long enough to have resulted in poor patient care for accident victims in West Cambria

- The cost of hiring the commercial service can be met by levying service fees on users

- Both West and East Cambria are similar in terms of traffic, weather and infrastructure aspects to draw such a comparison between the two

- Charging a service fee for ambulance use will not discourage people from using it

Missing evidence

- Proof that a considerable number of victims have suffered due to the "longer" response time of the volunteer service

- Proof that both East and West Cambria share similar traffic and weather conditions and have similar infrastructure to have equivalent ambulance response time

- Proof that people will not think twice before dialing for a commercial service knowing that will be charged a fee

- Hiring a commercial ambulance service will in fact not result in increased spending for the governing body and the cost will be compensated through service fee

Counter-examples

- What if West Cambria's volunteer ambulance service has in fact better survival rates for victims, despite a longer average response time?

- What if the difference between the average response times of the two services is not significant enough to have any substantial effect on patient care?

- What if West Cambria is more densely populated, suffers from traffic congestions, and experiences adverse weather conditions such as rain, snow and the like?

- What if hiring the commercial service proves to be a loss making exercise in light of high cost of operation vis-a-vis revenue incurred?

- What if people generally feel discouraged to call upon the paid service due to the expense involved?

The essay

The writer of an editorial column of a newspaper compares the average response times of the ambulance services plying in two regions – West Cambria and East Cambria. Since it has been found that the commercial ambulance service of East Cambria fares better than the volunteer service of West Cambria, the writer suggests abandoning the volunteer service in favor of hiring a commercial squad for West Cambria as well. This, the writer states, will result in better emergency care for patients of accidents and, in the process, fill the government coffers. In building this argument, the writer has drawn comparisons between two regions and two different kinds of services, without checking the merit of such a comparison.

The argument of the writer is riddled with flaws at several levels. First up, the writer has assumed that the average response time to accidents is the only factor that determines the merit of an emergency care system. It is very well possible that the volunteer ambulance service, though having a longer response time, is better equipped at administering first aid to accident victims than the commercial service of East Cambria. Secondly, even if one assumes that the two services are at par with respect to preliminary care provided and response time is the only deciding factor, there is no evidence in the argument that proves that victims of West Cambria have indeed suffered due to a delay in the arrival of an ambulance. In other words, it is only an assumption on the part of the writer that the response time of the volunteer service is long enough to have resulted in poor patient care of accident victims in West Cambria.

More basically, the writer's argument will fall flat if the comparison being drawn is unjust. It should be noted that the comparison is being drawn between the ambulance services of two different regions. West and East Cambria may well be miles apart and be as different as chalk and cheese in their infrastructure, traffic and weather conditions, making the comparison void. Again, assuming that the two regions are in fact similar at all such levels, it cannot be concluded for certain that operating a commercial ambulance service is financially viable for the exchequer in West Cambria. The writer suggests levying a service charge on users to help increase the revenue of the town. Besides being ethically questionable, the act may not necessarily meet the intended purpose. What if the cost of hiring and maintaining the commercial service is higher than what the government can charge from the people? There's also a possibility that people may hesitate in calling for an ambulance in case of emergencies due to the financial barrier. This may in fact backfire in providing better patient care.

Summing it all up, the decision to scrap the volunteer service and bring in a commercial ambulance service is hasty and flimsy. The writer should take note of other factors discussed above in comparing the two regions and the two services before deciding for one over the other.

4.31 Essay 31 (Perks Company)

> *The following is part of a business plan being discussed at a board meeting of the Perks Company:*
>
> "It is no longer cost-effective for the Perks Company to continue offering its employees a generous package of benefits and incentives year after year. In periods when national unemployment rates are low, Perks may need to offer such a package in order to attract and keep good employees, but since national unemployment rates are now high, Perks does not need to offer the same benefits and incentives. The money thus saved could be better used to replace the existing plant machinery with more technologically sophisticated equipment, or even to build an additional plant."
>
> *Discuss how well reasoned you find this argument. In your discussion be sure to analyze the line of reasoning and the use of evidence in the argument. For example, you may need to consider what questionable assumptions underlie the thinking and what alternative explanations or counterexamples might weaken the conclusion. You can also discuss what sort of evidence would strengthen or refute the argument, what changes in the argument would make it more logically sound, and what, if anything, would help you better evaluate its conclusion.*

Understand the argument

The business plan drafted at a board meeting of the Perks Company spells out the futility of offering extravagant benefits to the employees in light of high unemployment rates. The business plan states that such a package makes more sense at a time when it is difficult for the company to retain and attract good talent, and not when there are many unemployed people seeking jobs. The Perks Company can instead divert its funds to bettering its machinery or constructing a new plant.

Faulty assumptions

- High unemployment rates imply severe shortage of jobs

- Rolling back the employee benefit package will not take a toll on the motivation level of employees and their productivity will not suffer

- Unemployment rates are so high as to stop any major exodus of employees from the Perks Company despite the withdrawal of the incentive scheme

- High unemployment rates ensure availability of skilled workforce as well

- National unemployment rates reflect the unemployment rates in the Perks' industry

- The company indeed requires "more technologically sophisticated equipment" or an additional plant, and it can support these changes in all other respects

Missing evidence

- · A significant proportion of the unemployed are employable

- · Proof that employees will be equally motivated even without the employee benefit scheme

- · Proof that unemployment rates are so high that there are no attractive opportunities whatsoever for the employees to look out for

- · There are enough eligible candidates in the workforce that Perks can enlist in case of attrition

- · Proof that national unemployment rates are representative of the industry that Perks is engaged in

- · The Perks Company requires, and is ready to, augment its production through advanced machinery or a new plant

Counter-examples

- · What if the majority of unemployed are actually unemployable?

- · What if the employees slack in productivity owing to decreased motivation?

- · What if there are sufficient jobs in the market but few skilled people?

- · What if the unemployment rates in the Perks' industry are not that high after all?

- · What if the money saved from employee benefit scheme is insufficient for carrying out either of the two tasks envisioned?

The essay

The Perks Company has been offering an attractive package of benefits and incentives to its employees over the years. It is now being debated in a board meeting that the scheme should be discontinued taking into account high national unemployment rates. The rationale behind the move is that such a scheme is judicious only when there is an imminent threat of attrition to the company – that is when unemployment rates are low. Since presently, national unemployment rates are high, it is prudent to do away with the benefit program and instead redirect the funds for procuring technologically advanced machinery or building a new plant. The argument takes an over simplistic view of the situation and ignores various scenarios under which the above line of reasoning wouldn't hold water.

At the outset, the argument suffers from two inherent flaw that makes the entire reasoning go for a toss. High unemployment doesn't necessarily imply a high number of eligible candidates without job. Unemployed and unemployable are two different terms with vastly different implications. As is empirically true for many countries, a major proportion of the unemployed population is without job, not so much for lack thereof, but for its lack of skills. Hence, a high unemployment rate doesn't necessarily guarantee a pool of good talent for Perks to choose from. This makes it clear that the employees of the Perks Company, if they so desire, may not face a dearth of job opportunities outside. Secondly, it is likely that withdrawing the benefit scheme may impact the morale of the employees and their productivity may decline. This makes it amply clear that the company's objective of attracting and retaining good talent is insufficient.

Delving deeper, one can uncover many assumptions that can easily be challenged. To begin with, the argument assumes that the unemployment rates are so high that a substantial number of employees will not be able to leave the organization, even if they wish to. The argument further assumes that national unemployment rates are representative of the unemployment statistics of the industry the Perks Company operates in. It is a possibility that the Perks' industry is highly specialized and so there are very few people who have the skills required to be in the job. Such a scenario may completely change the unemployment stats for Perks. Lastly, even if one assumes that everything that the business plan suggests about scrapping the employee benefit scheme is right, it still doesn't ensure that the end purpose is met. It is envisioned that the saved money can be pumped into building an additional plant for the company or upgrading the machinery. There can be two problems that may arise. Firstly, it may be possible that the money saved off the benefit scheme doesn't match up against the investment required for undertaking any of the two. This maybe likely since upgrading machines or building a plant are mammoth projects that employ large amounts of money. Furthermore, even if money doesn't pose a problem, there may be other shortcomings, say, insufficient raw materials to be processed, not enough market to sell the increased production, not enough manpower to man the plant or machines, etc., that may make this move questionable.

In summary, the board needs to draw up a detailed cost benefit analysis of the employee benefit scheme and compare it with that of the advanced machinery/new plant to arrive at a decision on continuing the package. Merely basing it on national unemployment rates is myopic.

4.32   Essay 32 (Vista Studios)

The following appeared as part of an article in an entertainment magazine:

"A series of books based on the characters from a popular movie are consistently best sellers in local bookstores. Seeking to capitalize on the books' success, Vista Studios is planning to produce a movie sequel based on the books. Due to the success of the books and the original movie, the sequel will undoubtedly be profitable."

Discuss how well reasoned you find this argument. In your discussion be sure to analyze the line of reasoning and the use of evidence in the argument. For example, you may need to consider what questionable assumptions underlie the thinking and what alternative explanations or counterexamples might weaken the conclusion. You can also discuss what sort of evidence would strengthen or refute the argument, what changes in the argument would make it more logically sound, and what, if anything, would help you better evaluate its conclusion.

Understand the argument

An article in an entertainment magazine writes that a proposed sequel to a popular movie will surely be profitable. The reasoning for this argument is based on the fact that books based on the characters from that popular movie are consistently doing well in local bookstores. The argument cites the success of the books and the original movie as a guarantee for the profitability of the proposed sequel.

Faulty assumptions

- Revenues are commensurate with profits

- The readers of the books and the audience of the movies are nearly the same target group

- Sales trends in local bookstores are representative of other geographies

- Audiences are not already saturated and bored with the same characters and will lap up any content revolving around their favorite characters

- The new planned sequel will be well executed and will produce a finished product that will be popular

Missing evidence

- Evidence that the local sales trends can be extrapolated to a larger geography

- Evidence that the audience is not saturated and bored with the same characters

- Evidence that the new sequel will be good enough to be popular with the audiences

- Data that indicate that costs of producing the sequel will not equal or increase those of producing and marketing it.

Counter-examples

- What if the new sequel is not able to keep up with the high expectations generated by the original movie and series of books?

- What if the readers of the books are a different set of people from the audience for the movie?

- What if the audiences are actually bored of the same characters and would rather prefer movies based on new characters?

- What if the expenses in creating the movie outweigh the revenues generated by it?

The essay

Vista Studio plans to produce a movie sequel based on a series of books. These books have been consistent best-sellers in local bookstores. These books are based on characters from a popular movie. Because of the popularity of the movie and the books, the argument states that the sequel will be surely profitable. This is a specious argument that contains assumptions that have not been examined and is wanting of evidence that is pivotal to evaluating the soundness of the argument.

On the face of it, the argument looks convincing, but has certain assumptions that if proven unwarranted would invalidate the argument. First, the data on which the success of the books is evaluated is narrow. Whether that success can be extrapolated is something that needs to be further looked into. It is possible that the local bookstore success is not replicated elsewhere, perhaps, because there is an element in the book that is popular only in that locality. In which case, the decision to launch a sequel based on that book might be hasty and may not give the results that Vista Studios augurs. Further, the people who read books and those that watch movies can sometimes be a disparate demographic group, with little or no overlap. That a series of books is popular does not automatically translate into success of a movie based on its sequel. The books are based on characters of an original popular movie but the other elements, such as plot, of the books may be very different and may have been tailor-made to a book-reading population. The same plot when extended into a sequel may not have the elements that appeal to a movie audience.

Even if it were to appeal to a movie audience, any sequel has a distinct risk of failure due to comparison with the original book or movie that it is based on and can often be judged more harshly than a standalone movie because of the high expectations that the original book or the movie has generated. Another risk of a sequel is that it might lack the originality that is often required to stimulate the audiences and consequently its box-office success. Because it is based on characters already known to the audience, any sequel has a more difficult job than an original movie and can actually do badly instead of doing well. Further, even if the sequel were to do well revenue-wise, the same cannot be said for the profits which are actually a function of both the revenue and costs.

In conclusion, the argument reaches a hasty conclusion about the profitability of a planned sequel and requires more evidence and an examination of its assumptions to determine its validity.

4.33   Essay 33 (Magic Hat Brewery)

> *The following appeared as part of an article in a trade magazine for breweries:*
>
> "Magic Hat Brewery recently released the results of a survey of visitors to its tasting room last year. Magic Hat reports that the majority of visitors asked to taste its low-calorie beers. To boost sales, other small breweries should brew low-calorie beers as well."
>
> *Discuss how well reasoned you find this argument. In your discussion be sure to analyze the line of reasoning and the use of evidence in the argument. For example, you may need to consider what questionable assumptions underlie the thinking and what alternative explanations or counterexamples might weaken the conclusion. You can also discuss what sort of evidence would strengthen or refute the argument, what changes in the argument would make it more logically sound, and what, if anything, would help you better evaluate its conclusion.*

Understand the argument

In a trade magazine for breweries, an article proposes that to boost sales, small breweries should brew low-calorie beers too. This recommendation is backed by the following evidence: a survey of visitors to the tasting room of the Magic Hat Brewery shows that majority of the visitors asked to sample its low-calorie beers.

Faulty assumptions

- The people who tasted the low-calorie beers liked the taste

- The survey is valid, reliable and representative

- People who taste the beers actually end up buying them

- It is feasible, cost-effective, and practical for the small breweries to expand their product lines to low-calorie beers without adversely affecting their current products

- There are no better ways to boost sales by focusing on their present product line

Missing evidence

- Evidence that Magic Hat brewery has released correct survey results

- Evidence that the survey was scientifically formulated and administered

- Data that there is adequate demand for low-calorie breweries to warrant an increase in supply

Counter-examples

- What if the people who ask to taste the low-calorie beers do not actually like the taste?

- What if even if the visitors liked the taste, it does not translate into sales?

- What if the small breweries do not have the capacity to brew low-calorie beers?

- What if there are more cost-effective ways of boosting sales by focusing on the current product line?

- What if visitors to tasting rooms are usually tourists and purchasers of beers are usually locals?

The essay

An article in a trade publication for breweries recommends that small breweries brew low-calorie beers to boost their sales. The basis for this recommendation is a survey result published by Magic Hat Brewery. The survey of visitors to the tasting room states that the majority of the visitors asked to taste its low-calorie beers. The recommendation is based on perfunctory and insufficient data and jumps to conclusions without considering a lot of factors, making a recommendation that needs further evaluation to judge whether it is sound.

First, more data is required to understand the survey. How many visitors were there in all? What if the number of visitors was a small number, say five, out of which three asked to taste low-calorie beers? In this case, if the total number of visitors itself is small, it is not a sufficient number to extrapolate for other breweries. Even if the number of visitors is significant, are the demographics of the visitors to the brewery commensurate with those of the people who would actually buy low-calorie beers? It is possible that the majority of the visitors are tourists who actually will make only one-time purchases, if any at all. Further, what is the likelihood that those who ask to sample the low-calorie beers actually like what they tasted? It is possible that the low-calorie beers do not cater to the sensibilities of the beer drinkers who never take another sip of a low-calorie beer after tasting it once. And further what is the likelihood that those who like the taste actually go ahead and purchase the low-calorie beers?

Further, even if the low-calorie beers did well at the Magic Hat brewery, it is possible that the demographics of the visitors and clients at Magic Hat brewery differ substantially from those of other breweries because of factors such as location. It is possible that the Magic Hat brewery is located near a health-conscious locality whereas other breweries have clients who might prioritize price or taste and not necessarily calorie count. A low-calorie beer might be more expensive or less delectable than a usual beer and may then fail to capture the interest of other categories of clients. Moreover, even if the small breweries wished to brew the non-calorie beers, it may not be feasible due to factors such as limited space, stocking complexities, and increased costs of production.

In sum, further data needs to be garnered and the recommendation needs to be investigated thoroughly before it is considered as viable. To boost sales, the breweries might want to consider other methods such as expanding their channels of distribution, having alluring sales offers, giving membership privileges before considering expanding their product lines.

4.34   Essay 34 (Pageturner's profits)

> *The following appeared in a memorandum from the assistant manager of Pageturner Books:*
>
> "Over the past two years, Pageturner's profits have decreased by 5 percent, even though we have added a popular cafe as well as a music section selling CDs and tapes. At the same time, we have experienced an increase in the theft of merchandise. We should therefore follow the example of Thoreau Books, which increased its profits after putting copies of its most frequently stolen books on a high shelf behind the payment counter. By doing likewise with copies of the titles that our staff reported stolen last year, we too can increase profitability."
>
> *Discuss how well reasoned you find this argument. In your discussion be sure to analyze the line of reasoning and the use of evidence in the argument. For example, you may need to consider what questionable assumptions underlie the thinking and what alternative explanations or counterexamples might weaken the conclusion. You can also discuss what sort of evidence would strengthen or refute the argument, what changes in the argument would make it more logically sound, and what, if anything, would help you better evaluate its conclusion.*

Understand the argument

An assistant manager of Pageturner Books recommends following a particular practice by Thoreau Books – putting copies of its most frequently stolen books on a high shelf behind the payment counter – as a remedial for its decrease in profits and increase in theft of merchandise.

Faulty assumptions

- Books and merchandise are not being stolen by staff

- There is adequate security in place currently

- Putting the books on a high shelf will not adversely affect sales of those books

- People who steal books are only interested in stealing particular books and not any book in general

- A significant portion of costs are due to losses from stolen merchandise

Missing evidence

- Evidence that the books stolen are related to particular titles and not due to their location

- Data that losses due to stolen books and merchandise is substantial and will have major impact on turnaround of profits

- Evidence that Thoreau Books did not increase profits due to some other measure

· Evidence that the measure of keeping the specific titles on a high shelf behind the payment counter by Thoreau Books has actually managed to reduce losses due to theft without adversely impacting sales

Counter-examples

· What if the decline in profits is temporary and the new cafe and CD section will start bringing in increased profits soon?

· What if currently the losses due to theft are minimal and focusing on that will not have a major impact of profits?

· What if Thoreau Books increased profits due to some other reason?

· What if by making those specific books difficult to access, it actually deters people from purchasing them?

· What if even after taking this measure, people who steal books continue to do so with other easily accessible titles?

The essay

Pageturner's net profits have declined five percent and the argument proposes that to cut losses due to theft of books and merchandise, Pageturner should follow a practice adopted by Thoreau Books. Thoreau books put copies of its most frequently stolen books on a high shelf behind the payment counter and reportedly increased profits after that. The argument recommends that Pageturner adopt this practice to increase profits. The argument is weak in its current form and requires more evidence and examination of its assumptions to determine the argument's validity.

The argument begins by citing data about reduction in profits. The figure and its contributing factors need to be investigated further. Is the reduction in net profits due to expansion of space and will actually not impact next year's profits? Is the reduction in profits due to an increase in theft? If so, has anything changed to increase theft? Perhaps it is due to lack of adequate security measures such as a CCTV or security guards at the entrance or inadequate personnel at the store? Perhaps an employee is stealing books and merchandise. The real reasons that allow theft and the actual extent of damage due to theft need to be determined before a corrective measure is evaluated for its merits. What if losses due to theft are below the industry standard and are currently not making much of a dent on the profit margins? In that case, making books difficult to access can actually have an adverse impact on sales and hence on profits.

Further, it is also possible that the theft has less to do with specific titles and more to do with the location and accessibility of the books and merchandise. Even if the frequently stolen titles are made difficult to access, it is entirely possible that the miscreants continue to steal other books and merchandise that replace the shelves. Moreover, Thoreau Books may not be comparable with Pageturner, and any measures adopted by the former may not be suitable for the latter. What also needs to be determined is whether the accompanying increase in profits for Thoreau Books was truly due to the change in location of frequently stolen titles or due to some other measures also taken which might have positively impacted revenues or reduced costs.

To conclude, though blindly copying a competitor might be appealing, it would be fruitful to evaluate the recommendation specifically from Pageturner's perspective by examining further evidence and assumptions.

4.35   Essay 35 (Artificial sweetener aspartame)

The following appeared in the health section of a magazine on trends and lifestyles:

"People who use the artificial sweetener aspartame are better off consuming sugar, since aspartame can actually contribute to weight gain rather than weight loss. For example, high levels of aspartame have been shown to trigger a craving for food by depleting the brain of a chemical that registers satiety, or the sense of being full. Furthermore, studies suggest that sugars, if consumed after at least 45 minutes of continuous exercise, actually enhance the body's ability to burn fat. Consequently, those who drink aspartame-sweetened juices after exercise will also lose this calorie-burning benefit. Thus it appears that people consuming aspartame rather than sugar are unlikely to achieve their dietary goals."

Discuss how well reasoned you find this argument. In your discussion be sure to analyze the line of reasoning and the use of evidence in the argument. For example, you may need to consider what questionable assumptions underlie the thinking and what alternative explanations or counterexamples might weaken the conclusion. You can also discuss what sort of evidence would strengthen or refute the argument, what changes in the argument would make it more logically sound, and what, if anything, would help you better evaluate its conclusion.

Understand the argument

A trends and lifestyle magazine carried an article that states that it is preferable for people to consume sugar than to ingest aspartame, an artificial sweetener. The article provides two main reasons for the assertion – one, that consuming a high amount of aspartame can lead to weight gain, and two, that sugar, if consumed after at least 45 minutes of working out, can in fact help burn off calories. The article hence concludes that people consuming aspartame instead of sugar would find it difficult to meet their dietary goals.

Faulty assumptions

· People switching to aspartame from sugar all aim to lose weight through this habit

· The normal intake of aspartame for people falls under the 'high level' category, as mentioned in the studies

· Sugar, if not consumed after at least 45 minutes of exercise, will not have a greater adverse effect on calorie loss in people than consuming aspartame

· Taking aspartame after at least 45 minutes of exercise does not have an effect similar to that of sugar on the body's ability to burn fat

· Consumption of aspartame or sugar is the only factor that decides if people meet their dietary goals or not

Missing evidence

- Proof that the main motive of people switching to aspartame is to reduce weight

- Proof that people consuming aspartame as a substitute for sugar would end up consuming high levels of aspartame

- Proof that sugar wouldn't adversely affect people's diet goals when consumed before the 45 minute window

- Proof that aspartame too doesn't have the positive effect of burning off calories when ingested after 45 minutes of rigorous workout

- Proof that having aspartame along with undertaking other healthy habits will not achieve the same dietary results for people (as compared to consuming sugar)

Counter-examples

- What if people switching to aspartame do so for reasons other than losing weight?

- What if people end up consuming very little amount of aspartame and so the ill effects of having high levels of aspartame become immaterial?

- What if consuming sugar, when not accompanied by continuous exercise, has adverse effects on calorie loss far greater than the positive effects it has otherwise?

- What if aspartame too, when taken after a fairly sufficient time of exercise, enhances the body's ability to burn fats just as sugar does?

- What if, by making other changes in their dietary habits, people can achieve their diet goals with aspartame as well as they can with sugar?

The essay

The health section of a trends and lifestyle magazine features an article on why it is more prudent for people to go back to sugar than to have aspartame, an artificial sweetener. The article quotes the findings of two studies to show how aspartame can actually pull you back from your weight loss track by making you pile up calories, and how sugar can actually accelerate your body's ability to burn fat. The studies, of course, come with their share of disclaimers but the article goes on to build the argument by generalizing the findings for people at large – disclaimers notwithstanding – and concludes that aspartame is a bad choice for people looking to achieve their dietary goals.

Right in the beginning, the argument commits a blunder in assuming that all people who take to aspartame as a substitute for sugar do so for losing weight. It is very likely that there are other reasons for people to discontinue sugar and go for an artificial sweetener, say, for example, controlling blood sugar levels, being allergic to sugar or its components, or just aiming for better health. It is obvious that if there are individuals who consume aspartame for any of these reasons, the original argument of sugar being better than aspartame for it aids weight loss, falls flat. Conceding that weight loss is indeed the main motive for people to switch to the artificial sweetener, one can spot another flaw in the argument in the term "high levels of aspartame". The argument states that certain studies have shown that consuming high levels of aspartame makes you crave for more food and you may in fact end up consuming more calories than you hoped to cut down by reducing your sugar intake. Now, what is labeled high by the studies may be quite different from what people in general end up consuming. That is, it is likely that people only ingest small quantities of aspartame and hence this effect doesn't show up on them.

The article builds the argument further by stating that while aspartame can make you eat more, cutting down on sugar can leave people bereft of the calorie burning advantage that comes with consuming it after 45 minutes of continuous exercise. This point is questionable on two grounds. Firstly, it doesn't take into account the possibility that aspartame can also have a similar effect when followed by a rigorous exercise routine. Secondly, the argument is silent on the effects of consuming sugar immediately after a workout or without it. It is possible that sugar, when consumed in such a manner, in fact adds far more calories than it helps you burn after a workout. Hence, it is not logical to suggest that having sugar in place of aspartame is better in general, when the positive effect of consuming sugar is conditional.

Finally, the conclusion of the argument is also flawed in that it fails to take into account other factors that may affect how, when and if people meet their dietary goals. It limits the discussion to only sugar and aspartame and without any substantial evidence, ends up concluding that people who take aspartame are unlikely to achieve their dietary goals. It is possible that people can indeed lose weight while being on aspartame, provided they supplement it with other healthy changes in their lifestyle.

In summary, the argument picks and chooses instances that support the assertion without providing evidence that can vouch for the claim. It also fails to take into account other aspects that may affect the assertion. It is, in conclusion, a partial and limited analysis and needs to be substantiated further for the claim to be indisputable.

4.36 Essay 36 (Actor Robin Good)

The following appeared as part of a column in a popular entertainment magazine:

"The producers of the forthcoming movie 3003 will be most likely to maximize their profits if they are willing to pay Robin Good several million dollars to star in it—even though that amount is far more than any other person involved with the movie will make. After all, Robin has in the past been paid a similar amount to work in several films that were very financially successful."

Discuss how well reasoned you find this argument. In your discussion be sure to analyze the line of reasoning and the use of evidence in the argument. For example, you may need to consider what questionable assumptions underlie the thinking and what alternative explanations or counterexamples might weaken the conclusion. You can also discuss what sort of evidence would strengthen or refute the argument, what changes in the argument would make it more logically sound, and what, if anything, would help you better evaluate its conclusion.

Understand the argument

A popular entertainment magazine has dished out advice to the makers of the movie 3003 that they should rope in Robin Good to star in the movie if they wish to earn big bucks. This, however, will come at the cost of several million dollars for the makers as fee for the actor. The magazine's rationale is that since Robin Good has been paid this handsomely for working in movies that eventually ended up being big money grossers, his participation in 3003 can replicate similar success.

Faulty assumptions

- Concurrence of Robin Good's participation in a movie and its financial success implies a cause and effect relationship

- Robin Good was the sole reason for the financial success of his previous movies

- The makers cannot maximize their profits without Good's involvement in the movie

- Robin Good cannot be hired to work in the movie at a lesser price

Missing evidence

- Proof that the success of the previous movies can solely be attributed to Good's participation in the movie

- Proof that there is no other means for the movie to make big money except for having Good star in it

- Proof that Good cannot be convinced to lower his fee by any means

Counter-examples

- What if Good's participation in the movies and their financial success was merely a coincidence?

- What if the financial success of the movies in question was a cumulative result of various factors such as good direction, storyline, screenplay, etc.?

- What if the makers of 3003 can make even more money by investing in a better director, a great marketing campaign, or first-rate special effects, etc.?

- What if the movie's storyline and Good's character are both so engaging that he agrees to do it for a lower price than expected?

The essay

A magazine has come out with an article that claims to offer a piece of advice to the makers of a to-be released movie 3003. The article states that the producers of the movie can maximize their profits by bringing on board Robin Good, although they'll have to shell out several million dollars for this. The magazine backs its claim by bringing up the success of Good's previous movies when he was paid this handsomely. The argument is clearly skewed in that it fails to look at the possibility of Good's participation in his successful movies as one of the many factors that may be responsible for the said success.

The argument is a classic example of confusing correlation with causation. Just because the movies in which Good was paid a huge amount ended up being successful doesn't imply that their successes were due to Good's involvement or for the fact that he was paid a huge amount to star in the movies. Similarly, it cannot be deduced from this that every time Good is paid a huge amount to star in a movie, it will necessarily result in great financial success for the movie as well. Secondly, even if there's any truth to this causation, there's not enough evidence in the argument to say that this trend will definitely continue. In other words, even if one assumes that Robin Good did have any role to play in the success of his movies, the contribution of other factors cannot be discounted. Probably, the storylines of all those movies were great, the direction was excellent or they were simply marketed really well. It is very likely that those movies worked for all these factors put together, Good's participation included. As a corollary, it is also likely that the movie doesn't end up doing well despite all these factors contributing. This could be due to a lot of reasons such as the time of the release, a big sporting event happening at the same time, poor advertising, another equally good movie releasing simultaneously, etc. All in all, the argument lacks sufficient evidence to establish the intended cause and effect relationship between Good's participation in the movies and their subsequent successes.

Besides these very basic flaws in the argument, the magazine's claim can be challenged on several other grounds as well. For one, the argument nowhere provides proof that the only way that the makers can maximize their profits is by hiring Good to star in the movie. It may be possible that there is another even more bankable actor who can ensure similar success for the movie and may not charge several million dollars like Good does. Further, it is possible that Good himself agrees to star in the movie given, say, for the plot of the movie, the director, the remaining cast, etc. In summary, the argument is devoid of substantial evidence that can back the claims made by the magazine.

4.37   Essay 37 (University hospitals Vs. Private hospitals)

The following appeared in an article in the health section of a newspaper:

"There is a common misconception that university hospitals are better than community or private hospitals. This notion is unfounded, however: the university hospitals in our region employ 15 percent fewer doctors, have a 20 percent lower success rate in treating patients, make far less overall profit, and pay their medical staff considerably less than do private hospitals. Furthermore, many doctors at university hospitals typically divide their time among teaching, conducting research, and treating patients. From this it seems clear that the quality of care at university hospitals is lower than that at other kinds of hospitals."

Discuss how well reasoned you find this argument. In your discussion be sure to analyze the line of reasoning and the use of evidence in the argument. For example, you may need to consider what questionable assumptions underlie the thinking and what alternative explanations or counterexamples might weaken the conclusion. You can also discuss what sort of evidence would strengthen or refute the argument, what changes in the argument would make it more logically sound, and what, if anything, would help you better evaluate its conclusion.

Understand the argument

The argument aims to debunk the misconception that university hospitals are better than private hospitals by providing evidence such as lower success rate, lesser overall profits, fewer doctors, and underpaid medical staff vis-a-vis private hospitals. It also cites university doctors' research and teaching as an impediment in providing quality care to the patients. The argument uses all these points to establish that university hospitals provide relatively lower quality care to their patients as compared to what the other community or private hospitals do.

Faulty assumptions

- The performance of university hospitals in one region reflect the performance of university hospitals in general

- Lower success rate necessarily implies poor quality of patient care

- Number of doctors and profit made are indicators of the level of patient care for a hospital

- The kind and number of patients treated at both the kinds of hospitals is comparable

- Doctors undertaking research and teaching along with their regular job of treating patients are not able to do justice to the latter

Missing evidence

- Proof that the evidence cited for the hospital in question are true for all university hospitals

- Proof that hospitals with lower success rate also have lower quality of health care

- Proof that more number of doctors or a well paid staff can improve the quality standards of a hospital

- Proof that both kinds of hospitals treat patients with comparable diseases and are frequented by a similar number of patients

- Proof that undertaking research and teaching by the doctors come in the way of administering quality health care services to the patients

Counter-examples

- What if the other university hospitals have higher success rates than that of the private hospitals?

- What if the university hospital in the region treats patients suffering from far more complex diseases while the private hospitals are frequented by patients suffering from routine or known illnesses?

- What if research and teaching help the doctors acquire more knowledge in their field and in fact makes them more competent?

- What if other university hospitals have more number of doctors and a better paid staff than that of the private hospitals?

- What if profits, strength of doctors, etc. do not affect the quality of health care provided?

- What if the university hospitals are frequented by a far greater number of patients thus making the comparison unfitting?

The essay

A newspaper has published an article which claims that the notion of university hospitals being better than private hospitals is a misconception. To prove this claim, the article presents certain comparative evidence pertaining to the university hospitals in a particular area. These include lower success in rates in treating patients, fewer number of doctors in the hospital, lesser salaries for the medical staff and lower overall profits, in comparison to private hospitals. The article also brings in the fact that doctors of university hospitals are also engaged in research and teaching. Taking all these into account, it is concluded that university hospitals in general provide lower quality of patient care than community or private hospitals.

The argument suffers from many critical errors. The most basic and blatant of these is the author's use of evidence pertaining to university hospitals in a particular area to draw a conclusion generalizing for all university hospitals. The argument provides no evidence whatsoever that all that is stated for the university hospitals in the area in question is representative of university hospitals in general. Further, the argument states that university hospitals have a 20 percent lower success rate in treating patients as compared to the corresponding number for private hospitals. Now, this could have been a very valid point had the argument also supplied certain evidence in support of this claim. Since the argument is silent on the kind of patients that are treated in the university hospitals in comparison to that treated in the private ones, comparing the success rates of the two hospitals may not necessarily give a true picture. It is possible that university hospitals most often treat patients suffering from rare and complex diseases while the private ones only treat patients suffering from ordinary illnesses. This can hence explain the difference in success rates for the two hospitals and can justify that university hospitals do not necessarily provide inferior health care than what private hospitals do.

The argument tries to cement its claim that university hospitals provide no better care to patients than private hospitals do by citing more evidence such as fewer doctors being employed in the university hospitals, lower overall profits and lesser paid medical staff. Neither do these factors have any obvious link to patient care, nor is any evidence provided to establish that link. There's no reason why lesser number of doctors would necessarily provide poor care to patients. Similarly, overall profits may simply be low for the fact that they may be charging low from the patients. The same reason can also explain lower salaries for the medical staff. Hence, these three factors have no bearing on the quality of health care provided in the university hospitals. The argument talks of university hospitals' doctors diving their time between research, teaching and treating patients. Again, this evidence in no way proves that these doctors do a poorer job of treating patients than the doctors at the private hospitals. If this indeed has an effect on patient care, it has to be positive, for this may only better the doctors' knowledge of medicine and add to their experience.

Hence, the argument is weak for it fails to prove how and why the university hospitals in this region represent all university hospitals and that the evidence cited have any direct link to the quality of health care provided.

4.38   Essay 38 (Megamart grocery store)

> *The following is part of a business plan created by the management of the Megamart grocery store:*
>
> "Our total sales have increased this year by 20 percent since we added a pharmacy section to our grocery store. Clearly, the customer's main concern is the convenience afforded by one-stop shopping. The surest way to increase our profits over the next couple of years, therefore, is to add a clothing department along with an automotive supplies and repair shop. We should also plan to continue adding new departments and services, such as a restaurant and a garden shop, in subsequent years. Being the only store in the area that offers such a range of services will give us a competitive advantage over other local stores."
>
> *Discuss how well reasoned you find this argument. In your discussion be sure to analyze the line of reasoning and the use of evidence in the argument. For example, you may need to consider what questionable assumptions underlie the thinking and what alternative explanations or counterexamples might weaken the conclusion. You can also discuss what sort of evidence would strengthen or refute the argument, what changes in the argument would make it more logically sound, and what, if anything, would help you better evaluate its conclusion.*

Understand the argument

The management of Megamart grocery store has tabled a business plan that proposes addition of new departments and services on the grounds that this is the surest way to increase profits over the next couple of years. The business plan has drawn from the recent 20 percent increase in sales after the store added a pharmacy section. The management argues that customers are lured by the convenience of shopping under one roof and hence it is prudent to keep adding new sections to the store in order to increase profits.

Faulty assumptions

- Increase in sales implies increase in profits

- The 20 percent increase in sales over last year's is not natural for the grocery store

- The hike in sales is completely a consequence of the addition of the pharmacy section

- The proposed new sections are similar to the pharmacy section so as to have a similar (positive) effect on sales

- Adding these sections is financially viable for the store

- Customers will not flock to a competing store that specializes in one of the new sections and offers better prices

Missing evidence

- Proof that increasing sales will translate into increasing profits

- Proof that the addition of the pharmacy store is the sole reason for the increase in sales

- Proof that the proposed sections are all similar to pharmacy in business prospects and will result in an increase in sales

- Proof that the cost of adding these sections will not outweigh the increase in sales

- Proof that customers indeed only seek the convenience of one-stop shopping

Counter-examples

- What if increase in sales is accompanied by a proportionate increase in costs as well?

- What if the increase in sales was not a direct result of the addition of the pharmacy section?

- What if the proposed new sections do not have a market in the said area?

- What if it is very expensive to set up and diversify into some of these new sections?

- What if the customers rate value for money higher than the convenience of one-stop shopping?

The essay

The management of Megamart Grocery Store has come up with a business plan of adding new sections and departments in order to increase profits. This decision comes on the heels of a 20 percent increase in sales following the addition of a pharmacy section to the store. Basing this success, the management concludes that customers look for convenience of one-stop shopping and hence it makes sense to add a variety of sections to its grocery store. Such a move will give a competitive edge to the store and also help in increasing profits. Apart from the fact that the management confuses increase in sales with increase in profits, the argument also lacks logic in that it doesn't provide substantial evidence to support the proposed measures.

To begin with, the argument only states that there was an increase in sales after the store added a pharmacy section. This doesn't say anything about the contribution of the pharmacy section in the increased sales. Nor does this preclude the possibility of the increased sales coming from efforts in the grocery section such as huge discounts, addition of new stock, shut down of competing grocery store, etc. Simply because the addition of the pharmacy section preceded the hike in sales, doesn't mean that the two share a cause and effect relationship. Moreover, it is also likely that this 20 percent increase is not that big a number at all. Probably the store in general grows by similar percentages and the addition of the pharmacy store happened to coincide with the increase.

Examining the argument further, one can uncover various other loopholes. Firstly, increase in sales necessarily do not imply increase in profits. Setting up new departments and sections will incur costs and it is likely that the increased sales may not translate into increased profits. Secondly, even if one gives in to the fact the increase in sales can be owed to the addition of the pharmacy section, it cannot be guaranteed that the addition of the proposed new departments will also result in success. It is likely that the pharmacy and these other departments differ highly in terms of the business prospects they offer. It is also possible that setting up these departments doesn't prove financially viable for the store. Further, the area may not have the kind of customer demographic to which these new sections may appeal. Hence, one cannot for certain conclude that the addition of new departments will result in increased sales and/or profits. Finally, the premise that customers are mainly concerned with convenience in shopping is also unsubstantiated. The argument is silent on how customers will react to a specialty store opened next door that may offer a variety of products in a particular category at low prices. It is under these circumstances that the assertion of customers rating convenience as supreme will be testified.

The entire discussion boils down to the fact the management needs to take a closer look at what caused the increase in sales and whether this increase actually resulted in profits. The management also needs to assess if adding new departments and sections is cost effective and if these additions will indeed bring in more profits. Only when the management delves into all these aspects should the decision of adding new departments to the store be taken.

4.39   Essay 39 (Trends and lifestyles)

The following appeared in a magazine article on trends and lifestyles:

"In general, people are not as concerned as they were a decade ago about regulating their intake of red meat and fatty cheeses. Walk into the Heart's Delight, a store that started selling organic fruits and vegetables and whole-grain flours in the 1960's, and you will also find a wide selection of cheeses made with high butterfat content. Next door, the owners of the Good Earth cafe, an old vegetarian restaurant, are still making a modest living, but the owners of the new House of Beef across the street are millionaires."

Discuss how well reasoned you find this argument. In your discussion be sure to analyze the line of reasoning and the use of evidence in the argument. For example, you may need to consider what questionable assumptions underlie the thinking and what alternative explanations or counterexamples might weaken the conclusion. You can also discuss what sort of evidence would strengthen or refute the argument, what changes in the argument would make it more logically sound, and what, if anything, would help you better evaluate its conclusion.

Understand the argument

A trends and lifestyle magazine has commented upon the lack of concern among people these days towards regulating their meat and fatty cheese intake. To drive home the point, the magazine relies on the sheer variety of cheeses available with an organic foods store and also points to the financial success of a new restaurant, House of Beef. In the same breath, the magazine also cites the abysmal performance of an old vegetarian restaurant. All these points are intended to establish that people in general are not as concerned as they were a decade ago about monitoring and regulating their meat and fatty cheese intake.

Faulty assumptions

· Dietary habits of people in the area where the three stores are located are reflective of the dietary habits of people in general

· A wide variety of a product necessarily implies that people buy more of it

· Dull performance by Good Earth cafe is not due to the quality of food offered but due to the fact that it is vegetarian

· The success of House of Beef can all be attributed to the sale of red meat and fatty cheese items

Missing evidence

· Proof that the sample in question is indicative of the dietary habits of people in general

· Proof that the sale of cheese in Heart's Delight surpasses that of organic fruits and vegetables

- Proof that people do not visit Good Earth cafe because it doesn't offer non vegetarian fare

- Proof that House of Beef's owners have turned millionaires all due to the great business of the restaurant

- Proof that vegetarian items on the menu of House of Beef do not sell as well as red meat and fatty cheese items

Counter-examples

- What if the dietary habits of the people in this area are starkly different from the people in general?

- What if despite the high variety of cheeses on offer, organic fruits and vegetables sell better?

- What if the Good Earth cafe has failed to make good profits owing to its poor management?

- What if the success of House of Beef is in fact due to a very popular vegetarian dish in the area?

- What if the owners of House of Beef were millionaires before they started the venture or ear from other business ventures?

The essay

A trends and lifestyle magazine has opined that people today are less concerned about managing their red meat and fatty cheeses consumption as compared to what they were ten years ago. The magazine begins to validate this through the fact that an organic foods store offers a wide variety of cheeses, moves on to the fact that Good Earth cafe, a vegetarian restaurant, is not doing well financially, and a non-vegetarian restaurant across the street has millionaire owners. The magazine commits the blunder of generalizing the findings about the dietary habits of people of a region to that of people in general. It also measures the financial success of two restaurants to comment upon the dietary habits of people in that area and in general.

As mentioned before, there is a fundamental error in the reasoning of the argument in that it paints the entire population with the same brush since it assumes that the dietary habits of the people from that area are mimicked by people in general. Since the argument takes the example of three food joints all in the vicinity of each other, the population frequenting these places is likely to be from the same region. Moreover, the eating habits of people from this region may be entirely different from that of the general population. Further, even if one assumes that this generalization can indeed be drawn, the fact that people from the area in question have a general lack of concern in moderating their red meat and cheese intake is questionable. The argument first states a store such as Heart's Delight, which is mainly an organic fruits and vegetables store, offers a wide variety of high fat cheeses. This is intended to imply that the variety is owing to people's demand for such food. This is however an assumption that cannot be validated. It is possible that despite this high variety, the sale of fatty cheese is lower in comparison to organic fruits and vegetables on offer. The argument then cites the poor fortunes of the owners of a vegetarian restaurant implying that people of the area do not prefer vegetarian food. This claim also can be challenged. The fact that this restaurant is not doing well may be for reasons such as poor management, stiff competition, etc. which do not have anything to do with the dietary habits of the people. Similarly, the fact that the owners of House of Beef are millionaires doesn't prove anything. For all that the argument tells, the owners may have started as billionaires and may have now ended up being only millionaires! It could also be possible that they are earning well from their other business ventures. Moreover, it is also likely that their vegetarian fare does equally well or even better when compared to the red-meat and fatty cheese dishes.

In sum, the magazine makes an unsubstantiated claim based on the information from a limited and probably biased sample. It needs to reassess the dietary habits of the people in general and cover a wider sample space to derive conclusions of such general nature. Also, the fact that the financial conditions of restaurants can be related to the general ebbing concern for regulating meat and cheese consumption needs to be substantiated.

4.40 Essay 40 (Aurora company)

> *The following appeared in a memorandum from the president of Aurora, a company that sells organic milk (milk produced without the use of chemical additives):*
>
> "Sales of organic food products in this country have tripled over the past five years. If Aurora is to profit from this continuing trend, we must diversify and start selling products such as organic orange juice and organic eggs in addition to our regular product line. With the recent increase of articles in health magazines questioning the safety of milk and other food products, customers are even more likely to buy our line of organic products. And to help ensure our successful expansion, we should hire the founder of a chain of health-food stores to serve as our vice president of marketing.""
>
> *Discuss how well reasoned you find this argument. In your discussion be sure to analyze the line of reasoning and the use of evidence in the argument. For example, you may need to consider what questionable assumptions underlie the thinking and what alternative explanations or counterexamples might weaken the conclusion. You can also discuss what sort of evidence would strengthen or refute the argument, what changes in the argument would make it more logically sound, and what, if anything, would help you better evaluate its conclusion.*

Understand the argument

The president of a company that sells organic milk proposes two measures. First, diversify and start selling products such as organic orange juice and organic eggs. This measure is to profit from the trend of growth in sales of organic food products. Second, hire the founder of a chain of health-food stores to serve as vice president of marketing. This measure is to ensure a successful expansion.

Faulty assumptions

- The trend of sales growth will continue upward

- Sales of organic foods is proportionate for all organic products and not led by a few specific products

- Diversifying product line is the only way to profit from the favorable sales trend

- Magazine articles about food safety actually influence consumer purchase choices

- Founder of a chain of health-food stores would be willing to join them as a vice president marketing

Missing evidence

- Evidence that the supply of organic goods does not already exceed their demand

- Evidence that a founder of a chain of health-food stores is actually competent in marketing

- Data about sales trends of the products the company might consider adding to their product line

- Data that the growth in sales trends is in the geographies where the company currently supplies or can supply its products

- Data about the performance of the existing product line vis-a-vis the market trends

Counter-examples

- What if the growth trend is not sufficient to warrant an expansion?

- What if the growth trend is primarily due to a few products which are not the products the company currently offers or will offer in the future?

- What if the company is not able to offer the products at a price that will attract customers as well as be viable for the company?

- What if the current product line itself is not doing well and the company is not in a position to capitalize on the growth trend for reasons such as quality or pricing?

- What if the founder of a health-food store is not experienced in marketing or not interested in joining the company?

The essay

The president of Aurora—a company that sells organic milk—cites the trend of tripling of sales of organic products over the last five years as the grounds for a proposition to diversify the existing product line to include products such as organic eggs and organic orange juice. The president also cites the recent increase of articles in health magazines questioning the safety of milk and other food products as the basis for customers being more likely to buy the company's product line. The president also recommends that the company hire the founder of a chain of health-food stores as vice-president marketing to spear-head the proposed expansion. The argument makes tenuous recommendations on the basis of perfunctory data, unexamined assumptions, and missing evidence.

The data about sales is insufficient. Greater details are required not only about the demand as per different organic products but also the supply of the same. It is possible that the sales of organic milk products (the current product) or organic orange juice and organic eggs (the proposed product line) are not on an upward trend, and the upward trend is primarily due to one or few products. Perhaps also, this growth in sales might be endemic to particular locality where the company does not operate. If it is so, then expansion would not benefit Aurora. It is also possible that even though there is a growth in sales that growth might be met or even superseded by supply by other companies offering better or cheaper organic products than those offered by Aurora. In this case, any growth in sales may not actually benefit Aurora but will be lapped up by the more competitive companies.

Further, the president cites the spate of articles questioning the safety of milk and other food products as a reason for increased likelihood of people buying Aurora's products. There is a huge jump from the evidence to the conclusion here. A major assumption here is that the articles are actually read by a substantial amount of people. Second, that reading the article galvanizes the reader to take action. Third, this action involves switching to organic products Fourth, the organic products the reader will shift to will be Auroras.

Another suggestion made by the President involves the hiring of the founder of a health-food store as Vice-President Marketing to ensure the expansion takes place smoothly. The argument assumes that a founder would be an expert in marketing, rather than merely a person who funds the project and borrows marketing expertise. Further, the argument assumes that the founder, given that he is a marketing maven, would be actually interested in joining Aurora as a marketing vice-president.

In conclusion, the suggestions made by the president require further investigation in terms of further data and examination of the underlying assumptions.

Chapter 5

Talk to Us

Have a Question?

Please email your question to *info@manhattanreview.com*. We will be happy to answer. Your questions can be related to approaches, analysis of prompts, essay topics, or challenges in writing 6.0 essays.

Please mention the page number when quoting from the book.

Best of luck!